MW01593741

DEAR MAMA

Through The Eyes of a Child

SYDELLE N. RICHARD

Glory Books Publishing, LLC

Cedar Hill, Texas

www.glorybookspublising.com

Sydelle Richard

Published by
Glory Books Publishing, LLC
P.O. Box 2373
Cedar Hill, Texas 75106
www.glorybookspublishing.com

ISBN 0-9786235-0-9

Printed and bound in the United States of America

Table of Contents

DEDICATION

This book is dedicated to My Family.

To my husband Keith – I Love You

To my children Skylar and Keith II my pride and joys and my undisputed #1 fans

To my two brothers who have loved me from the beginning

To my mother who I am finally getting to know and love

To my Aunt Wanda who loved me as her own

To my best friend and cousin Wynema who ALWAYS believed in me (thank you!)

To my little cousin Meka (not MeMe) I love you

I love you all so much. We have all gone through a lot, and continue to endure even more; my prayer is that all we have endured will draw us closer together.

ACKNOWLEDGEMENTS

First and foremost, I acknowledge my Father in Heaven who grants me new grace and mercy everyday; He who comforts and calms me, who sustains me and strengthens me. Without Him, I have nothing and am nothing.

I would like to thank Dr. Frederick Haynes III. I will never forget your kindness, wisdom, support and guidance. You are awesome, inspiring, and gifted. You are a wonderful mentor and friend. I love you Pastor Haynes, thanks for everything. May God continue to smile upon you and grant YOU that perfect peace that surpasses all understanding.

To Mr. and Mrs. Karry D. Wesley – you two are truly inspiring. I have never met two more humble servants. I am so very grateful for your kindness and thoughtfulness. Words cannot express my appreciation.

To Robyn, Sheila, Dena, Angelia, Andrea, Sondra, Trae and Milt: thank you for believing in me and showing me true friendship. I love you guys!

To my NEW family: Mom, Dad, Shirley, Brenda, Beverly, Michelle, Glenda and Karen thank you for making Skylar and me feel loved and for welcoming us into your family. I love you.

For Somere Sanders: Thank you so much for taking time out of your life for me.

Sydelle Richard

What lies ahead of us, and what lies behind us, are tiny matters compared to what lies within us.

-RALPH WALDO EMERSON-

...greater is he that is in you, than he that is in the world.

- 1 John 4:4-5 (King James Version of the Bible)

INTRODUCTION

*W*hen I started writing this book, it was for my benefit. I started writing in 1999 shortly after my grandmother passed away. At the time, I was going through a divorce, starting a new job, purchasing my first home and trying to cope with her death. When my grandmother passed away, our relationship was not what it had been in the past. I had a lot of questions regarding my childhood and hers. There were things I wanted to have conversations about, but the timing was never quite right.

After I had my house built, she was going to come and visit with me for a few months. I had determined that would be the perfect opportunity for us to sit down and talk. I wanted to strengthen the relationship she and I had but it wasn't to be. My grandmother was supposed to arrive at my house on July 19, 1999; but tragically, she was killed in a car accident on July 17 of the same year.

I will never forget the day. I was riding in my car with my daughter and one of her friends. One of my cousins called me; she was trying to sound cheerful as she asked if I had spoken with my grandmother. I told her that I had not; she then informed me that there had been an accident. Immediately I started making plans to call the hospital and find out how she was, but my cousin then told me that she wasn't at the hospital, that she didn't survive the crash.

My heart sank. It felt like a nightmare. My grandmother had been somewhat sickly for most of my life. She was diabetic, and she suffered from a number of lung diseases, but I had just spoken with her the day before, and she was fine. I was trying to drive, but I started shaking uncontrollably and I could not stop. I pulled over and put my head down. I remember thinking I had to keep things together because I had the children in the car with me. I wanted to scream, but I just wiped the tears away as fast as I could to keep them from asking questions, which would have made me cry even more. That day, I knew I would be away from home most of the time, so I had forwarded my home phone to ring on my cellular phone. When my cousin found out I was driving, she panicked and started calling people to come and get me.

I composed myself and drove the girls home. By the time I got home, I was not crying, I was in a state of disbelief. I could not believe the news. I had spent most of my life trying to make her proud of me and now after I had just purchased my home, one of my proudest accomplishments, she would not be there to share it with me. The only decorating I had done was in her room. I wanted her to feel comfortable and welcomed. I wanted her to be there to share in my joy. She had been sick so often and there were many times that I tried to prepare myself for her death. I would mentally try and calm myself while imagining the worst. But even in my dreams, it was never sudden. There was always time to say good bye. In my worst nightmare, she and I still had our last conversation. There was time to prepare; but reality turned out to be more harsh than my imagination would allow.

Everyone was calling to see if I was OK, but my wellbeing was the furthest thing from my mind, I was really concerned about my mother, Satchell. Satchell was in prison at the time my grandmother passed away. I knew I would have to be the one to give her the news. The next morning, I got up early and drove to the prison. I cried most of the way. I felt so sorry for her because I knew she would feel a lot of guilt for the pain she had caused my grandmother. I felt that she would feel cheated in that she finally wanted to get her life together and neither of her parents would be there to share in her success.

When I arrived at the prison, the guard noticed that I had been crying. She asked me if I was bringing a death message. I told her that I was. She immediately summoned the warden who informed me that they typically did not allow such messages to be given in person, but since I had driven such a long way, she would allow it. She informed me that guards would be standing by and that if my mother made any sort of emotional outcry they would terminate the visit and make her return to her cell. The warden felt she could not risk having Satchell's outcry cause a commotion while prisoners were freely walking around during visitation.

I sat in the waiting room, trying not to cry taking deep breaths to compose myself. When Satchell came out – she immediately knew something was wrong because the guards were standing by and because I could not look at her. As she approached, I stood up and she just asked 'what happened?' The guard told her 'She has a death message – and you cannot have an emotional reaction or else the visit will be terminated'.

My mother acknowledged what the guard said and asked me who passed away – I told her that Mama had been in a car accident and that she had died. I had always called my grandmother 'Mama' because she raised me, and she was the closest thing to a mother that I had known for most of my life. When Satchell heard this, she just closed her eyes tight and sat down. I was hurting for her. I felt so bad; there was nothing I could do to console her. I could not hug her and I could not speak because I would start crying. I just sat there, holding her hand across the table.

Finally, once she had composed herself, she asked how the accident had happened. I was not sure, and all I had heard was that she crashed into a building and that there were no skid marks, she never hit the brakes. When I heard that, I immediately thought she had committed suicide.

I felt awful that she had died alone, but even worse was the thought that my grandmother had taken her own life. I was not about to share that with my mother. I did not want to upset her anymore than she already was. We later found out that she had gone into cardiac arrest before the crash, but at the time, all I could imagine was the worst possible scenario. Our visit lasted a few hours, but once the time was up, I did not want to leave her, I could not imagine how she would feel having to go back to a cold, dark cell; unable to grieve the loss of her mother. The drive back home was just as dreadful as the drive going. With that done, I called the warden and started making arrangements for my mother to attend her mother's funeral.

Throughout the process of making final burial arrangements, nothing seemed real. I was in denial. I still had the urge to call out to my grandmother. As I walked through her house, I could still feel her presence. I kept thinking I would eventually wake up and things would be normal again. Even on the day of the funeral, I could not help walking back to her room, expecting to see her. There are many things about the day of the funeral that I do not remember. I remember the day in general, July 21, 1999; but most of the details are a blur. I could not tell you whether it was sunny or cloudy, warm or cold; I cannot remember. I was in shock, I was angry, I was sad, but more than anything, I felt all alone. There were hundreds of people at the funeral, but none of them shared the relationship I did with my grandmother. I loved her dearly; and yes, we had many disagreements, but when all was said and done, at the end of the day I was in her corner and she was ALWAYS in mine.

I honestly had no idea where to begin the grieving process, because I had not yet accepted the fact that she was gone. I was still in denial, which I guess is the first step, but that was as far as I could go. Needless to say, there were a number of things I still wanted – needed to say to her. That is when I started writing. It had helped in the past to at least get things off my chest; but in this case, the more I wrote, the more pain I felt. As I wrote, I realized there were a lot of unresolved issues and feelings I had bottled up inside. I stopped a number of times because it was too painful to continue.

This project has taken a number of years to complete, and it has definitely been a very emotional journey, but ultimately, I am glad that God spoke to me and encouraged me to share my story. I'm glad that He placed the right people in the right place just when I needed them. I realize now that He has been strategically orchestrating my life since my humble beginnings and I am forever thankful.

1

HUMBLE BEGINNINGS

I was sitting and talking with my grandmother.

I was sitting on the floor while she was sitting on the bed, brushing my hair. It was dark outside, but the light from the moon was so bright it illuminated the room. The curtains were pulled back and I was staring out the window as I spoke. I was talking to her about my grandfather, Matthias. My grandfather was one of a kind. He was strong, handsome and knew something about almost everything under the sun. I was telling her I had been thinking about him a lot and I really missed him since he passed away. My grandfather 'Daddy' as I called him had passed six years prior. The entire time I was talking, she never responded, she simply smiled and listened with an occasional nod. I went on and on about how much I loved him and how I couldn't stop thinking about him.

Finally she asked, 'what do you think that means?' I assumed she was asking why I thought I was thinking about my grandfather so much. I just responded saying 'I guess it means that I should cherish the time I have with you because you are all I have left.' Before I could finish my statement, I looked up and she was gone. She had vanished into thin air. That's when I woke up.

Then I realized she too was no longer alive. My grandmother passed away as well. It was only a dream. It was a dream so real I could still smell the fabric softener in her clothes. I could feel the warmth of her body near me. It was so real because I wanted so much to have her with me.

My grandmother was taken from me without warning. I just woke up one day and she was gone. I still have the urge to pick up the phone and call her. I never had the chance to say good-bye. Even today I can still feel her presence. There have been many times I have cried, praying for just one more day with her. During those times, God sends me a comforter. It is during those times I have the dreams.

I have had many wonderful dreams about my grandfather as well. The difference is when I dream about my grandfather, I know he has passed away – even in my dream. I dream of him as if he is a guardian angel who has come to visit me for a while. Sometimes, when things are extremely rough, I dream of him sitting on a park bench, waiting for me to stop by, and then he reaches out his arms and embraces me; that's it. He just gives me a big hug, and it feels so real. His hands and arms feel so strong, like they can protect me from anything. I wake up and I can feel him holding me. I know it's God, but at the time, it feels like I have my daddy back for just a moment, and it carries me through.

On the other hand, when I dream about my grandmother, she is always alive. I dream of her at our old house where I grew up. I dream of her laughing and talking loud as she often did. I never dream of her as if she has passed on like my grandfather. I'm not quite sure what the difference in my dreams means. Part of it I'm sure is because her death was really hard for me to accept. As I mentioned, I have yet to properly grieve, I have yet to let go of her. Of course when I awake, there is a sadness that fills me, but for a brief moment, I have her, even if it is only in my dreams.

I have many unresolved feelings about both of my grandparents; I would give anything to have just one more week with them, one day or even an hour. I loved them so much and even after all of these years I still think of them every day.

I was raised by my grandparents; but by the time I started to realize what a real sacrifice they had made, they had gotten pretty old, and my time with them was limited. My childhood was far from a walk in the park, but I realize now that there was a purpose behind my pain. I spent so much time full of anger, resentment and distrust that I failed for a long time to see the blessing which is just being alive.

I was born the youngest of four children and the only girl. I have three older brothers; Dominique, Alonzo and Bob. Dominique, who is the oldest, is 5 years older than I am. My mother, Satchell, had me when she was 19 years old. I am the youngest of four children, you do the math. A mother of four at age 19, and what's worse is that she was also a widow.

You see, my brothers all have the same father, his name was Gabriel King. He was killed in Vietnam while my mother was pregnant with Bob, the youngest of the boys. During the time of the war, the US military did not require you to enlist if you had minor children to care for. In fact, their policy was not to accept young men in that situation. At the time however, my mother and Gabriel were separated, she had left him.

They were forced into marriage when she became pregnant at age 14. My mother, as I understand things, did not want to be married, they were both very young; but she succumbed to the pressures of family and got married. Shortly after, she became pregnant again with my brother Alonzo. I don't think my mother was in love with her husband. She just ended up in a situation that she didn't know how to handle.

At 14 years old, her mind was not yet mature enough to be a wife and mother. After a while, she decided to leave. I am not sure of the circumstances surrounding the separation; I just know that she left. When she finally reached the point that she could not stay with him any longer, he could not bear to live without her, and ultimately, he would not.

When Gabriel initially tried to enlist, he was denied because of his young family. He was determined to get away from my mother because he couldn't stand to be near her and not be with her; so he continued to persist in his efforts to join the military until the US Army finally received him in. In a last desperate act to reconcile with my mother, he asked her once again to take him back but she refused yet again. Satchell says that her final rejection was more than he could stand and as an act of angry passion, he raped her, impregnating her with the youngest of the boys, my brother Bob.

By the time Bob was born Gabriel had already been killed in the war and my mother's maternal instincts had died with him. She was a seventeen year old widow with a child on the way and her grip on reality was slowly starting to slip. When Bob was born, she gave him away. He was a manifestation of a horrible act that was forced upon her; a constant reminder of the pain of her last encounter with her deceased husband. She gave him away to my Aunt Laverne. Aunt Laverne welcomed Bob and the check the government would send to take care of him.

It seems that after Gabriel died, what ever causes a mother to love and nurture her children died in Satchell. It was as if a switch had been turned off. I have often asked what actually pushed her to that point. It isn't natural for a mother to have no regard for her children. She has yet to answer my question.

At that time, she had three sons, no husband and virtually no conscience. She left the two oldest boys with my grandparents and went out in search of what ever she thought she had missed by being such a young bride and mother. She started to run with the wrong crowd and ended up in jail time and time again.

Then comes baby number four – me. By the time I was born, Satchell's days of being a mother were far removed. She left me when I was five or six months old, with the baby sitter who was one of her younger cousins. Basically a little school girl who thought I was cute. She left me and didn't return; at least that is what I was told.

So apparently there was some sort of debate about who would keep me. There was an older cousin who didn't have any children at the time; an aunt who didn't have a daughter and finally, my grandparents, who already had my two oldest brothers. The difference between Bob and me was that since his father had been killed in Vietnam, the US government would take care of him, at least until his 18th birthday. Me, on the other hand, no one knew who my father was. To be perfectly honest, I don't think my mother is certain to this day of who my father is. With me, I would be an added financial burden. My grandparents finally came to my rescue and gave me a home. My mother claims it was the promise of her sending money that convinced my grandmother to keep me. Of course, I will never know the truth.

  The good thing was, at least I had a home. The bad thing was that our home served as the after-hours liquor store and weekend gambling shack. I can remember people coming to our house in the middle of the night for beer and alcohol. My grandfather would buy large quantities of liquor and sell it at a premium after the liquor stores had closed. When someone would ring the doorbell, he would grab his handgun before going to the door. The person would usually stand outside until he brought back what he or she wanted.

  On the weekends, men would come from all around the Texas panhandle to gamble at my grandparent's home. By the time I made it home from school on Friday, the house would be filled with loud, boisterous, dirty old men.

My two oldest brothers, Dominique and Alonzo were a bit older and because they were boys, they had quite a bit more freedom than I did, so they were gone a lot. There were times when I would be alone, but sometimes during the school year and almost every summer, my cousin Sabrina would stay at my grandparent's with me. She was my best friend. I loved Sabrina. Throughout all of my life she is the one person who has always been there for me. Even when I was at my worst, she stayed and put up with my rotten moods and negativity. She usually stayed with her mom or dad during the school year. I think I resented her for having caring parents. Although her parents didn't live together, she knew them and she knew they both loved her.

She and I fought a LOT when we were children; mostly because I was angry at her and the least little thing she would say or do would set me off; but no matter how mad she made me, I always wanted her around. I hated being there by myself – with all of those nasty men.

Sometimes, while the men were gambling, Sabrina and I would put on my grandmother's high heeled shoes and strut across the hall, switching our behinds, right where they could see us. Anyone who wasn't at the gambling table could look down the hall and see us. I was six and she was five at the time. It really seemed harmless; we were just playing a game. The ironic thing is that they would sit there and watch us. Neither of them ever told us to stop, and never said anything to either of my grandparents.

They watched us as if they were enjoying the show. We didn't dress up, we had on our regular little kid clothes; we just put on the shoes and tried to walk sexy – like in the movies. I will never know how that little show fascinated 50 year old men, but it did for several months.

Long after that, I heard a man speaking about young girls and how they dress and act. He said they were trying to dress all grown up, but they were not mentally mature enough to handle what they were inviting. If only someone had sat me down and had that talk with me that summer – I may have been spared the years of despair that were to follow.

After the summer, Sabrina went to her Dad's for the school year. I didn't want her to go. At least when she was with her mom I could still see her. Anyway – I stopped playing the game with the high heeled shoes. It was no fun to play alone, but it was already too late.

I'm not sure if they would watch me to see when I went into the bathroom, but somehow, one of those dirty old men always ended up in there with me. Sometimes they would back out after getting a peek. Other times, they would try and hold me in there and touch me.

I can remember one Saturday, the very next summer, I was seven years old. Everyone was outside except me. I went into the bathroom and just as I was getting ready to walk out, Mr. Dickson – one of my grandparents' best friends walked in. I was already dressed, but he forced me back in and started trying to kiss me and touch my private parts. I started to cry and he let me go. I ran to my room and sat on the floor in a corner, rocking back and forth with my head between my knees. He stopped by my room and threw some money at me and told me to be quiet. I never told anyone. I was afraid of him, and I couldn't stand to be around him. He always looked at me in a way that filled me with disgust; and he tried to touch me anytime he had the opportunity.

He was one of the 'high rollers' of Dimmitt. He made quite a bit of money and wasn't married, so he was always paying women to have sex with him. I guess he thought throwing his money at me would make everything OK. Once I was around sixteen, he told me 'You ain't no baby no more'. Like I was supposed to just do whatever he wanted. I did not like him AT ALL. He tried to use his money to lure me to his house.

Once he gave me a fifty dollar bill and told me to stop by his house later. I looked at him and shook my head. He left and I went to the movies. The next day I saw him and just stared at him, daring him to say anything about the money. He did that for a whole summer – the next time, he said, 'You didn't come last time – this time I'll be waiting for you'. I was thinking 'Sure – OK (weirdo)'. I never went; I just took his money all summer long.

He was pure evil and just about everyone knew it. But things were different back then; especially for blacks. At that time, money equaled status even more so than today, because not many black people had money. For that reason, everyone tolerated Mr. Dickson's vulgar language and actions. He had money. His money didn't faze me. I still didn't want anything to do with him, even as a child.

It all started with the bathroom incident when I was seven. That was the beginning of the end. It seems that from that point on, I was the automatic target of every dirty old man in the panhandle of Texas. Every time I stayed over at a friend's house I was always groped by either an older brother or their father. It never failed, I would wake up at night sometimes and there would be a strange man lying next to me trying to touch me.

Sydelle Richard

2

INNOCENCE TO SHAME

*A*fter that summer, my life was never the

same. I have thought back time and again, trying to figure out why things happened the way they did. I was far from being an early bloomer. I was very skinny with no breasts or curves anywhere in sight. I was just a normal little kid or so I thought. I finally had to just accept what God allowed. Even though those things were horrible – I would have preferred to have dealt with those random acts of immorality than to have endured the six year ordeal that began later that same summer.

The biggest difference between the little malicious acts and the 6 year ordeal was that it involved someone I loved and trusted. He had spent the greater portion of my life making sure that I loved and trusted him. He could have written a manual on how to be a pedophile.

The man was a close friend of my entire family; maybe that's why they let me spend so much time with him. He taught me how to cook and drive and even to sew. At seven years old, I could make pancakes, cornbread and even bake a cake – all from scratch. He always let me sit on his lap and drive. I never, ever felt endangered or afraid. I thought he loved me. I guess in his sick perverted mind – he actually did love me.

His name was LD Pedoster, and I guess he figured that seven years was long enough to wait. I started to wonder if maybe he had heard about the things the other men had done to me and wanted to be a part of it. Nevertheless, with him it was different. I had a loving relationship with him and he eased me into his dirty little hands.

LD was like a father figure. He stopped by my grandmother's house every morning and they would have coffee. I would get excited when I would hear his voice and I would run in and jump in his lap. He would take me out to the farm and while he was working, I would ride along with him on the tractor. When he went out of town, he would stop by my grandparent's house and pick me up. I loved going on our road trips. He would buy candy and soda and we would play games the whole way.

When I was nine years old, LD took me on a trip. We went for the weekend to Childress, Texas. He had family there and we went to visit. That was the first time he let me drive. He let me sit on his lap and steer the car. I was so happy. I remember smiling so hard my cheeks hurt. He kept telling me to relax my arms and not hold the wheel too tight. He would have me practice pulling out into traffic. 'Make sure you look to the left first' he would say. After a while we pulled over and he slid the seat all the way up. He got in on the passenger's side and I was in the driver's seat all alone.

First we went out into an open field. I practiced turning and going in a circle. I could never go backward because I could not see over the seat. LD kept telling me how well I was doing and how proud he was of me. He used to always tell me that I was smart and that I was going to make something of myself. He said he could see the little wheels turning in my brains when I was trying to figure something out. My grandparents were a little older than him, and my grandmother didn't have near the patience, so he took me places and did things with me, when they couldn't. My grandfather worked long hours and he was usually tired when he came home from work. He still made an effort to play with me once he was home, but LD usually took me out on Saturday while my grandfather was still at work.

I could hardly believe I was driving all by myself! I could not wait to tell my cousin Sabrina that I had driven. After we practiced in the field for a while, LD told me to turn onto the road. It was a country road with very little traffic, so he felt confident that I would be ok. As I was driving, a bee flew in right through the window. I started freaking out and screaming, LD talked to me and calmed me down. He told me that he thought the bee had flown out the window. His voice was so calm and soothing, that it took away the fear. Five minutes or so later, I could hear the 'buzzzz' of the bee. I kept telling LD that I could hear the bee. He dismissed it as my imagination. Then all of a sudden, the bee flies right in front of me and onto the front dash. I let go of the wheel and dove over onto LD in the passenger's seat. I was screaming 'The bee, the bee!!!!'

Once he regained control of the car, he pulled it to a stop, found the bee and killed it. Then he began to laugh uncontrollably. He said 'I guess I should have believed you when you said you could hear it'. He laughed on and off about that incident for the remainder of the trip. And when he finally dropped me off back at my grandparent's home he started in again while he was telling them the story. He just kept saying 'I hear it.' They all laughed at me for weeks about that little incident.

The times I shared with him were priceless. I shared experiences with him that no one else in my family was willing or able to share. He seemed to take a genuine interest in my well-being. The fact that my real father was no where in the picture probably made it easier for me to cling to LD. My grandfather was awesome, but he worked a lot. He was the sole supporter of our family. LD seemed to always have time off. I'm not sure how he managed that, but he never seemed to work much. When he did work, he would often stop by my grandparent's home on the way and pick me up. I would ride with him for hours on the tractor. He always wanted me around, with my mother in and out of prison so much and my father completely missing, I loved receiving the attention from him. He made me feel special. My cousin Sabrina had her mom and dad and I had LD.

Never in my wildest dreams did I imagine him having ill intentions toward me. As a kid, I completely trusted him as any other child would have in my position. He started making little comments about how pretty I was. I guess to see how I would respond. I was a bubbly little girl. Every little girl wants to be told they are pretty. He would often sit me on his lap while we were watching television. Still, it didn't seem strange or out of the ordinary in any way. Looking back, it is just hard for me to fathom how someone could completely take advantage of a small child who had complete faith in him.

The reality is that all of the trips, candy, TV time and every other time I spent alone with him was part of his demented plan. He wanted my complete trust. He wanted me to love him. He knew that my trust in him would allow him to control me and ultimately protect himself. A stranger being manipulative and calculating would have been more understandable; but this person was like a father to me. Or so I thought.

What I took to be a loving relationship, he used as part of his scheme to molest me. I can remember the very first day it started – it is still very vivid in my mind. I was seven years old. We were at LD's house and he had started cooking dinner. We had not long come in from working in the garden. While the food was cooking – he was sitting on the couch watching television. I was running around the coffee table in a circle.

Each time I would run by, he would lift his legs and I would jump over. I was laughing and having a lot of fun. It was so innocent. I was laughing and playing and all the while, he was plotting. After a while – he would grab me and kiss me. He kissed me on the lips, but I didn't think anything because it was LD and I knew he wouldn't hurt me. After he would kiss me, he would let me go and I would just jump up and start running around again just as any other seven year old little girl would have.

The kisses became more and more frequent and finally, he put his tongue in my mouth. I really didn't know what was going on, but again, I jumped up and started running. I remember him asking me how I felt about the kiss. I didn't really know how I was supposed to feel and I just replied and said 'I don't know'.

That was my first intimate kiss. I was seven. Honestly, at the time, I didn't feel weird or bad or anything about what had happened. I never thought he would do anything that would hurt me. I loved him.

That day, he told my grandmother that he wanted me to spend the night with him so that I could help him in the garden early the next morning. My grandmother allowed me to go. Why did she let me go? Why would she let me spend the night alone in a house with a 60 year old man with no wife or children? Nevertheless, I went. I wasn't hesitant at all; I was actually a little excited. I don't remember having stayed away from home prior to that night, except at Sabrina's house. That night, after my bath – I fell asleep in LD's bed. When I lay down initially, he was on the sofa; but at some point during the middle of the night, he came into the bedroom. When I woke up – he was on top of me. I was too afraid to scream. I didn't know what was happening. I remember trying to wake myself up thinking I must have been dreaming. Then I realized he was actually on top of me. I could hardly breathe because he was so heavy.

He was groaning and moving around on top of me and he kept calling me 'baby'. Then he started kissing me; first on the lips then all over my body and finally between my legs. I had my first orgasm at age seven. When he finally finished, I felt terrible, there was an awful feeling between my legs. I realized that he wanted what all of the other dirty men wanted. I was very sad and even more confused. I had experienced something that I was incapable of fully understanding. Not only did I not understand what had happened, I didn't feel that I could talk to anyone about what had happened.

The next morning before he took me home, he told me that he loved me and that I could never tell anyone what happened because they wouldn't understand. He said that if my grandfather found out, he would kill him and they both would be gone – he would be dead and my grandfather would be in jail. I never told anyone, at least not verbally, but I was never the same. That night had just been the beginning.

Year after year – things progressed and got worse. He would frequently perform oral sex on me; and I was sleeping at his house at least one night each week. He would usually wait until I was asleep before he started to fondle me, but sometimes he would just grab my hand and put it on his crotch and say 'see how you make me feel', indicating that I had caused his erection.

During the summer, he would pick me up during the day and take me out into a field in the country, just long enough for him to have an orgasm and then drop me off like nothing had happened. My life had changed so drastically. I was no longer the bright-eyed energetic, innocent child I once was.

When things initially started, I was confused, but I never thought LD would do anything to hurt me; by the time I realized that what was happening was wrong, things had progressed so far that I felt ashamed that I had let it happen; and he was constantly reminding me of the consequences if I were to have told anyone. By that time, I had no doubt that my grandfather would kill him. The whole thing was hard to process, because even in the midst of these sexual acts, he still acted as a father figure. He still taught me things, he even disciplined me. I didn't know how to respond toward him. On the one hand, I was starting to hate him. I would often lash out at him, saying things that probably warranted a whipping, but of course he wouldn't dare. On the other hand, some of my fondest memories to that point had been with him. I still loved him. This secret affair went on from the time I was seven years old until just before my thirteenth birthday. It was more frequent during the summer months, but he still managed to sneak in a few weekend visits during the school year.

I started to wet my bed at night. I can't begin to count how many beatings I got for wetting my bed, but how could I tell them that I had nightmares in the middle of the night, too afraid to move. I could feel him on top of me even in my dreams. The sad thing is that not one person was concerned enough to investigate and find out why the bed wetting started.

I was in 2nd grade before I started to wet the bed. No one took into consideration the fact that in all the six years prior, I had not had one night-time accident. Why would a 7 year old all of a sudden start such a habit? No one asked, I just got a whipping almost every morning. Satchell was the worst. She was hardly ever around. She would be away for months at a time, but she was guaranteed to find some reason to give me a whipping whenever she came to town; and my bed wetting usually gave her an excuse. Even if I had gone for weeks without an accident, the minute I knew she was coming into town, it always started back. I was afraid of her.

Sometimes she would tell my grandparents she was whipping me because of my bed wetting, but while she was hitting me, she would say things like 'That's for getting Alonzo in trouble.' My brother Alonzo and I used to fight a lot, but my mother adored him. He and I, being typical kids would often try and get each other in trouble – but if he told our mother Satchell, she always found a way to get me back.

I started to resent my brother Alonzo. I couldn't stand to hear his voice. He always made fun of me – which I now realize that he had no idea of the things I was dealing with, but at the time – he seemed only to be adding drama to my already plagued young life.

I hated everything – mostly myself; but I always had to smile and be pleasant around my grandparents' friends, most of whom had at least said something out of line to me at one point or another. Even my mother seemed to hate me. She was just mean for no reason; and when she did spend time with me, it was usually because my grandmother guilted her into taking me someplace. I remember once when I was nine years old, she whipped my butt because I didn't clean well enough for her behind the toilet. It was just another excuse. I didn't understand why she didn't like me; but that's how I felt most of my life.

Once she took me with her for the weekend. The first night, we went to some night club in Amarillo, Texas. She left me in the car, in the middle of the night in a dark parking lot with people going in and out – most of whom were drunk. While she went in to party, I sat in the car and watched the people – trying to stay out of sight. When she finally came back, she had a man with her. When they got in the car, she made me sit back while they made out in the front seat. The sad thing was, even at my young age, I knew exactly what they were doing.

When we got to her house, she locked me in her bedroom and that's where I stayed for the remainder of the weekend. As horrible as it sounds, it was probably one of the best weekends I had ever had. If I hadn't been there, I would have been with LD. She didn't really talk to me, but she would buy me McDonald's for breakfast, lunch and dinner. There was also a bathroom adjacent to her bedroom, so it was like I had my own little castle. I watched cartoons and ate McDonald's the whole weekend – it was great.

Later, I found out that Satchell had been selling and using drugs in the front room, which explains why I was locked in the bedroom. At least none of the men could get to me. That weekend passed all too quickly, soon I was back home, back to LD.

By that time I was nine years old, and LD told me he was making me the woman of his house. He said that none of the other women would act right and that he was just going to keep me there more and make me his woman. By then, I could cook almost anything. I could even drive a tractor. I had to mature fairly quickly. During the summer months I basically lived at LD's house. He would buy me little things, but mostly, he would give my grandmother money for letting me help him.

He just came in one night and started ranting and raving about how all the other women around were no good and didn't know how to treat him. He said he was tired of dealing with them. Then, he sat me down and said 'You know what? I'm just going to make you the woman of my house'. 'How does that sound?' he asked. I smiled and said 'OK'. I wanted to cry. I wanted to scream, but I didn't know what to do. I didn't feel there was anyone I could talk to. I thought both my grandmother and my mother would blame me for letting it happen. I KNEW my grandfather would kill him. I had no one to talk to. So there I was, nine years old trying to act like a grown woman as the 'pretend wife' of a sixty year old man. I did it. I cooked and cleaned for him. I satisfied him sexually. I confirmed his manhood. I'm not sure how a sixty year old man allowed himself to be mentally married to a child, but it happened. There was something in him, that I still don't understand, but it seemed to justify his actions. He bought me things and he gave my grandmother money, so I guess he thought he deserved to have me.

A couple of years later, when I was going into the 6th grade people started teasing me about being with LD so much. There was this girl, sort of a bully, in 8th grade, which she was supposed to be in 10th grade but she had been held back a couple of times. Her name was Miona Lakely. Miona was big and fat and smelt like dried blood. It was like she was on her cycle from birth and reused the same pad over and over. That's about the best way I can describe the odor. I knew her because her father, Mr. Lakely, was a good friend of my grandmother's. He would come over and gamble and sometimes bring Miona with him. One day on the playground, Miona started making fun of me, saying that I was sleeping with an old man. She started taunting me saying that LD and I were going to have a baby and get married. She said she heard her dad talking about it with someone. Miona told everyone on the playground that LD was doing things to me. I was very angry and even more embarrassed. I started yelling things back at her and finally we decided to meet after school to settle things. Please keep in mind that I was very skinny and 11 years old; this girl was BIG, even for her age, and she was around 15. Everyone thought I was crazy. I didn't care; I just wanted her to shut up. So we met after school and after the usual trash-talking, the fight began.

Somehow, my brother Alonzo had heard about the fight, he just kept telling me he was going to beat me up if I didn't hit her. I started hitting her, and somehow ended up on top of her. I just started hitting her in the face as hard as I could. Of course, my brother was egging me on more and more, but the odor was unbearable; I thought I would suffocate. Once the 'battle' was over, she left and I ran home to disinfect. She never brought LD up again – at least not when I was around, so I guess it was worth it.

A few weeks later, my Aunt Sarah, Sabrina's mom, started asking me questions about LD. She asked me if he had been trying to touch me. I lied to her and told her that he had only touched my breasts. What breasts? I don't know. She kept asking 'is that all?' I just told her that was it. I was scared and embarrassed; I just wanted everything to go away. I didn't want anyone to know. I started to wet my bed again; 12 years old and wetting my bed at night. I hated my life. Apparently my aunt said something to LD because he stayed away for a couple of weeks.

I loved my Aunt Sarah. She was always around when my mother was away. She wasn't like a mom, but more like a big cousin. I used to laugh watching her and her friends dance to the 70's R&B music. She was really a lot of fun. Of course there were days when she would yell and cuss, just as my grandmother did, but that was to be expected. That was all I knew. I was thankful that she asked about LD, but I was afraid he would be angry with me for telling her that he touched my breasts, which was nothing compared to the actual truth.

Things calmed down for a while, but soon, LD was back to his normal self and I was back at his house almost daily. He told me that I should thank him for protecting me while people were attacking him about what they thought was going on. By now I was approaching my 13th birthday; and up until this point, most of my life had been filled with guilt, shame, embarrassment, pain, anger and disappointment. There were however, three significant events that stood out as rays of sunshine among the dark clouds.

The first major event was my introduction to Jesus Christ. When I was about six years old, my grandparents took me to church with them. That is the only time I ever remember them going to church. It was a special occasion – someone very popular was coming to town. There had been a lot of talk among the adults, but of course children were not allowed in the room when they were talking, so I just got bits and pieces. I knew it was a big deal and I begged my grandparents to let me go with them. Sabrina wanted to go too, but they said they couldn't put up with both of us so only I was allowed to go. The church was packed and everyone had on their very best clothes. I sat between my grandparents, fully amazed. I remember the man saying that God would be a 'father to the fatherless and a mother to the motherless'. I remember thinking 'that's what I need'.

Prior to that point, I had never prayed, nor had I seen anyone pray. I had no idea why everyone was bowed, and I didn't bow, I just looked around with my eyes wide open; all I knew was that I wanted to know more. The next week, I asked my grandmother if I could go to church. There was a church right down the street from our house. That Sunday morning, she woke me up early and off I went.

From that point on, I was there every time the doors were open, sometimes before the Pastor. No one in my family went with me, but I didn't care. Sometimes, my grandmother would wake me up early to fix breakfast for my brothers before I went, but I didn't care. Sometimes, I had to run all the way because I was being chased by stray dogs, but I didn't care. It was the only place I felt truly safe. I learned how to pray, and talk to God. I prayed to God as if he were my earthly father. I loved Him. I loved that He loved me, even knowing all of the ugly secrets I had hidden in my heart.

I knew that no matter what happened the rest of the week, at least on Sunday and Wednesday, I would have a little peace. The pastor was Reverend

Alex Jamison, he was a really nice man; very old fashioned. He loved my curiosity and he was always willing to share. He had no idea about my personal life, but I thank God that he was a true man of God and not like the other perverts I had encountered.

He and I spent a lot of time together. I had a lot of questions and he was always eager to answer. He would sometimes be tired and yawning, but he would sit there and talk to me. He would just say 'I'm not tired; just need some fresh air – that's why I'm yawning'. He tried to convince me that he yawned only because he needed more oxygen. All the while, his eye lids were closing more and more with each passing minute. He was a good man. I will never forget the kindness he and his family showed me. I spent a lot of time alone with him, but he never said anything out of line; and he never tried to touch me. That was how I learned to judge men, when I was a child, the nice men never tried to touch me.

The second major event occurred when I got my ears pierced. It seems small, I know; but I was about six years old and my mother took me. Although my grandmother made her take me – she was actually nice. I remember having a big smile as I was walking through the mall with her. I was so happy just to be with her. It wasn't like we spent the whole day together. We drove from our home town to Amarillo, which took about an hour. She didn't really talk to me on the way, but it was just her and me – I couldn't ask for more. I was excited just to be with her. I felt special.

When we got to the mall, she asked me if I wanted to get my ears pierced. I was like 'YEAH!!!' It was almost too good to be true. We found a place and although I was nervous, I knew I couldn't let her know, I didn't want to do anything to upset her. When the lady shot the earring through my ear, it burned a little, but I wasn't about to say anything. I didn't cry or even flinch for that matter. I wanted her to be proud of me; and I think she was. She didn't say much, but she didn't yell at me. She did make it a point to tell me that she would beat me to death if I lost one of the earrings because they were real diamonds. That scared me a bit, because I knew she meant it; but at least for a while, it was like I had a real mom.

The third most significant event of my childhood happened the Summer I would turn 13 years old. A couple of weeks before my birthday my grandfather came to me and told me that I could not go back to LD's house. He said that he knew that LD would try something once I turned 13, if he hadn't already. Maybe he had started to sense something, I really don't know.

One day after school, he just called me out to the backyard and told me he didn't ever want me going back to LD's house. I guess he relayed the message to LD and my grandmother because I never had to go back. God had answered my prayers.

3

BRIGHTER DAYS

*A*fter my thirteenth birthday my life changed

significantly; at least on the surface. Somehow, God

had allowed me to block out the past years of shame

and guilt. I think the years were so painful, that my

subconscious didn't want to remember. I still saw LD

almost everyday, but the memories of what he had

done were suppressed to the point that I never

thought of them. There were still a few occasions

when I ended up at his house and he would say things

or touch me, but honestly, I didn't mind. It was still a

relief to not have to be his 'wife'. Having to endure the occasional touch was bearable. He made a comment once when I was in high school about my breasts being so small. He said if I had stayed around him, he would have made sure that I had large breasts. I just laughed it off. When my grandfather told me that I would not be spending time with LD like I had been, a burden was lifted. It allowed me to handle the comments and perverted glances because I knew my interaction with him would be limited. All of the past incidents were blocked out.

I'm not sure how it happened. I guess there are occasions when things are so grim and traumatic that it would do more harm than good to remember. God knew that at such a young age, it would probably have destroyed me to have to relive those moments day in and day out. Maybe I was just so relieved that it was over that I allowed myself to act as if nothing ever happened. I think LD was relieved, I really believe he wanted me to forget, and that explains why he started so early. He probably felt that as time passed, I would not have memories of the things he had done to me as a child. He almost succeeded. I went on with my life as if nothing had ever happened. It was as if all I remembered were the good times and the good things he taught me. All of the horrible acts were hidden someplace deep inside.

My 8th grade year was the start of better days. Prior to that year, I had just gone through the motions of everyday living. Between third and seventh grade things were probably at their worst. I lied A LOT! I was always making up stories about everything from why I was spending so much time with LD to why my mother was always away, even about who my father really was. I lied about practically everything.

When I was in third grade, I told my grandmother that if I got 100% on my spelling test on Thursday, I didn't have to go to school on Friday. My brothers were so angry. They kept trying to tell my grandmother that I was lying, but she didn't believe them. She told them things could have changed since they were in third grade.

Every Friday I could hear them pleading with my grandmother to make me go to school. That episode went on for about four weeks. I had three day weekends for a month! Even more interesting was the fact that she never asked to see my spelling test. I was intelligent, but I didn't make 100's on every exam, but she never asked and I didn't volunteer the information. As long as she didn't wake me on Friday morning, I knew things were OK.

Everything was going well until we had parent-teacher conferences. My Aunt Sarah had to go because of course, my mother Satchell was no place to be found. I remember so clearly watching my Aunt Sarah and Ms. Kohl, my teacher, sit at the front of the class at Ms. Kohl's desk. I remember them talking about what a good kid I was, and how well I was doing. I had near 100 averages in every subject except social studies- which we did on Fridays. Although I still had an 'A' average, Ms. Kohl expressed concern about me missing so many Fridays.

My heart dropped into the pit of my stomach. My aunt looked at me on the front row and then back at Ms. Kohl and says 'Sydelle told us that if she made 100's on her spelling test that she didn't have to go to school on Friday'. Ms. Kohl turned a shade of red not yet discovered by Crayola. She stood up and peered down at me. It looked as if she had grown at least five feet taller. Then, while all of the class was staring, she yelled, 'SHE SAID WHAT?!?" I just put my head on my desk. I thought I would never see my 9th birthday. 'Get in the hall!' she yelled.

I was so frightened that the embarrassment of all of my classmates staring didn't faze me a bit. In the hall, she kept asking me why I had told my family that lie. I told her that we didn't really do anything on Fridays so I thought it would be OK. She was furious. To be honest, I don't remember my aunt saying anything; she just stared at me. Ms. Kohl told me that if I missed one more day of school, she would fail me. What a relief, there were only a few more weeks left in the school year and no mention of a principal or paddling.

Even at home, I didn't get a whipping. I don't remember anyone saying anything, except my brothers teasing me. I was getting it for everything else, but for this – nothing. I think they were shocked that an eight year old child could concoct such a tall tale. So of course, I was on my best behavior at home and at school for the next three weeks.

Even with that, looking back, I just wanted to be home in my room. I felt safe there; in my room – with no one else around. I had so many emotions rolling around and at the time I was really confused. You would think that would have been another smoke signal for someone. First the bed wetting, and then skipping school at eight years old, what could be next?

The irony is that I had loved school prior to that summer. Before I was old enough to attend school, I would beg my grandfather to let me go with my brothers. So when I finally turned five, I was so excited. My first week was awesome. I remember crying because I wanted to go to school everyday, not just Monday through Friday.

My first teacher, Ms. Higgins was wonderful. She always gave me extra candy! She gave LOTS of hugs! I could hardly wait to get to school to see her. During nap time, she would lie with me on my cot. My grandmother didn't want me sleeping on the floor with a towel, so she bought me a small cot and Ms. Higgins would lie down with me until I fell asleep. I loved school. Everything was wonderful until that horrible summer that stole away my childhood innocence.

Afterwards, everything changed and I started to act out things I couldn't express in words. No one saw it as a cry for help, but more as me turning into my mother; spoiled and selfish.

Thank God for that glorious 13th year. After that, my grandfather became my hero. I had always loved him, he was a good man. He worked hard and took care of the family. I loved him dearly.

He and my grandmother would argue a lot about his drinking. My grandfather was a drunk – not necessarily an alcoholic, but definitely a drunk. He drank a lot and he gambled every weekend, but he was so nice. He wasn't the type of drunk who was loud and abusive. He didn't spend his whole check on alcohol. He still paid the bills. He was just drunk, nothing else changed. His demeanor was still calm and fairly quiet; he was still a nice person. His motor skills were a little, well, a LOT out of whack, but other than that, he was fine.

He worked hard Monday through Friday, maybe having a few beers in the evening; but Friday night - beware. Friday and Saturday night he would get drunk – every weekend. I don't mean tipsy – I mean falling down, passing out drunk. Even with that in mind, I still wanted to be with him. I would follow him anywhere. My grandmother used to get so upset with me because I always wanted to go with him whether he was drunk or not. She would get so upset because we were in so many accidents, I can't begin to count them all; but it never bothered me. The thing was, along with his intoxication, there was also his desire to be a race car driver.

My grandfather was notorious for driving fast. When he was sober, it wasn't as much of a big deal, but when he was drunk, he was out of control. I remember once, I was in the front seat and my brothers were in the back. At that time, seat belts were not required, so I was on my knees looking out the window. My brothers were crouched down in the back seat and they kept saying 'Daddy slow down'. I wasn't nearly as concerned as they were, but I should have been, because before I knew what happened, 'WHAM!" We had run into the back of another car – AGAIN.

This time I was thrown into the dash of the car. My mouth hit the dash and I was bleeding pretty badly. My brother Alonzo kept telling me that all of my teeth had fallen out and then I panicked even more. There were police cars everywhere. I don't know what happened to the people in the car that we rear-ended. The police came and took statements from witnesses and needless to say, they took my grandfather to jail; but only to let him sober up. He was home in no time.

A nice man that I didn't know carried me all the way to my grandmother's house. She was livid. When my grandfather finally made it home, she really let him have it. She kept telling him that he was going to kill me. That was probably the most angry I had ever seen her. It was an awful accident, and had it not been for the grace of God, I would have been hurt a lot worse. But even that didn't stop me from wanting to ride with him. I got right back in the car with him the very next day and was ready for action the next weekend. I think a part of me just wanted to try and keep him safe. There wasn't much I could do, but I would try and sober him up.

Sometimes when we would finally make it back home, he would be too drunk to move. He would just fall asleep in the car. It was only by God's grace that we ever made it home. I would sit in the car, sometimes for hours, trying to wake him and get him inside. He would laugh and say, 'Rabbit, you're the only one who loves me'. He always called me rabbit because he said when I was born I looked like a little baby rabbit squirming around. As drunk as he would be, him saying that made me feel special.

Mostly, I would try and get him in before my grandmother saw him. She would get so angry with him and start yelling and cursing. I hated to hear her talk to him that way.

The craziest thing is that my grandmother had also been a heavy drinker. In fact, she drank so much that her liver was severely damaged. The doctors told her that her next drink could kill her, and she never took another drink. Afterwards, she couldn't stand the smell of alcohol and even more so, she hated being around drunks, especially my grandfather. In retrospect, I can understand why she would get upset with him. I would not want a husband who was out every weekend getting drunk.

At the time however, all I saw was my daddy. He endangered the lives of my brothers and me almost every weekend. On top of that, he would often lose money and she HATED that. If there was one thing that I knew my grandmother loved, it was money. I don't remember her ever having a job, but she was definitely a hustler. Someone was always paying her for something. LD would often give her money for letting me help him in his garden. She was always looking for a way to make another dollar.

My grandfather on the other hand, didn't seem to care as much. He worked because he had to provide for the family. He gambled because he liked to gamble. I don't think the actual money was as important.

He was just a great man. He would ride bikes with me; I mean, imagine a sixty year old man on a little girl's bike. And the stories he would tell. He once told me that he used to pole vault – without a mat. He said he would just land on his feet every time. I believed him for the longest time. He said that when he played basketball, he had range out of this world. He said that as soon as he crossed the half court line, he would be lighting up the net and the whole team would just head back the other way. That story cast a little doubt in my mind, but only because I thought I was the greatest basketball player and I couldn't imagine him beating me.

Although I must admit, I would never have thought a sixty year old man could run as fast as he could either. I tried to run from him once when he was going to whip me. He reached for the belt and I took off out the back door. The next thing I knew, I felt a strap of leather across my legs. How in the WORLD did he catch me?

I was the fastest kid on the block. He was laying leather with every stride; and he was keeping up with me stride for stride, I was honestly amazed. Then, just like in the movies, I fell. That was all she wrote, he beat me until HE got tired. Needless to say, I never tried that again. Even after he whipped me, I can never remember being mad at him; at least not for very long. He was the kind of person everyone loved.

My grandmother was another story. I loved her dearly, but I didn't realize that until I was older. She was very strict with me. My brothers did basically whatever they wanted; but me, I had different rules. I was a girl and girls couldn't do the things boys did. I think teenage girls go through some sort of rebellious stage. Mine didn't hit until I was a senior in high school, but it was not pleasant.

All I wanted was a little freedom. I was a good kid, straight A's, National Honor Society even Student Body President. I did everything I was asked to do, but when I wanted to go out on a date or go to a dance, I had to first get the OK from my older brothers. The thing was, if it was a person they didn't like or an event they may have been attending and they didn't want to see me there, they would tell her it wasn't a good idea for me to go; and of course I would have to stay home.

I think maybe she was trying to protect me and keep me from turning out like my mother; and I truly understand that, but, I was not like my mother. My mother was the type who was too smart for her own good. She was also beautiful. Beauty and brains are an awesome combination when used properly; but in her case, she seemed to only use it to take advantage of people. She would laugh saying how she could get her friends to do anything she asked when she was in school. She thought it was funny.

Because of her appearance, she got a lot of attention, some positive and some negative. Men loved her and spoiled her. My grandfather was one of the main culprits. He would do anything she asked. Not because of her beauty, but because he loved her so dearly. His love for her was stronger than any pain she caused him by her mischievous acts. Unfortunately, all the love in the world didn't seem to be enough to save my mother from herself.

Sydelle Richard

DANGEROUS BEHAVIOR

$\mathcal{A}$s I got older, the gambling started to bother

me more and more; probably because I could never

have friends over on the weekend. In Dimmitt, where I

grew up, there weren't very many black families. By

the time I was in high school, there were only two

other Blacks in my grade and neither of them were in

any of my classes. I was the only black on my

basketball team and in any honors club or class I

participated in. The bottom line is that I didn't have

many black friends. They would have at least had somewhat of an understanding of how I lived.

I brought one of my white friends home, her name was JaTonne; she was in shock. 'Is that legal?' she exclaimed. Needless to say, that didn't happen again. The bad thing was that most of my white friends had at least one prejudice person in their family; be it an aunt or distant cousin – a grandparent or even a parent – so going to their houses and interacting with their families on a regular basis always left me as a target, bound to run into the bigot of the group.

In JaTonne's family, it was her grandmother. I don't think her brother was too fond of her hanging out with a black girl, but he didn't bother me much; but that grandmother – she did not like 'coloreds'. The funny thing was that her husband, JaTonne's grandfather was just the opposite - he loved me. He called me his little 'chocolate drop.' It was so much fun watching the grandmother squirm in her skin that I didn't mind all of the attention from him.

JaTonne and I used to go by their house just to see her grandmother turn red. She never said anything to me, always cordial, but she would tell JaTonne how she didn't like 'coloreds'. She would have steam coming from her eyeballs just watching her husband run around me like a little kid. Her mother would laugh at us and tell us we were going to give the old lady a heart attack.

JaTonne was really a good friend. I hung out with a lot of people, at various points throughout the year, but she was one of my closest friends. Dimmitt was a very small rural town and at that time, interracial dating was not happening; so I ended up being the best friend instead of the girlfriend. It bothered me at times, but I stayed busy with sports and other activities so I didn't spend much time thinking about it.

The thing with many of my white friends was that I was always more of a back-up. Meaning, if one of them were upset with their 'regular' best friend, they always chose me to hang out with; but as soon as things were smoothed over, they went back to being buddies and I went back to my second-base role. Once I figured out what was happening, it didn't bother me. I mean, I was always included in everything. I was one of the most popular girls in the school; I just didn't have a clique so to speak. There were a lot of other people I hung around and their immediate families accepted me and did things my grandparents couldn't do and my mother wouldn't do.

The Parson's used to let me go out on the three-wheelers and dirt bikes. I LOVED that. Marcie, their daughter was also one of my good friends. She was great, but some of her cousins made me a little uncomfortable. For instance, instead of saying vinegar, they would say vinigger; and then they would all burst out with laughter, even Marcie. I hated that, but that was just a part of it. They wouldn't dare say 'nigger', but to joke about it I guess made it OK for them. The Oaks, on the other hand, they were really good to me. I can't say that they were around many blacks before me, but I always felt at home at their house.

I was friendly to everyone – and I hung out with various types of people – White, Hispanic, geek, popular, short, tall – it didn't matter. I decided to be my own person and not worry about trying to fit in with one group. Peer pressure didn't bother me because I knew that ultimately, I would have to answer for myself regarding my actions, and some things just weren't worth sacrificing. In the long run, it made my high school experience more enjoyable.

I stopped trying to fit in and concentrated on being me. I was Miss Dimmitt High School, elected by the entire student body – no other Black girl had received that honor. Those were some of the best years of my life. I felt loved and respected – just for me. I was happy, but still not joyous. As happy as I thought I was, looking back I was still crying out.

By the time I was in high school, Satchell was an alcoholic and a drug addict. She had been in jail more times than I care to count and even served a term in prison. In fact, there were periods when the only time I would see her was when she was locked up. My grandmother would always make me visit her. I hated going to the jail, but my grandmother didn't want her to be upset so she would make me go. The ironic thing is that my mother was always accusing my grandmother of trying to take her place, when in all honesty, had it not been for my grandmother, I would have given up on my mother long before I did.

After a while, especially once I was older, I just got tired of the broken promises and the constant incarceration. I hated having to always lie to the police when they would come looking for her. She would hide in the closet and have me tell them that she was not there. Then, once they were gone, she would come out as if nothing had happened and disappear for months. Even with that, at the time, I was young and still wanted her around, so I would cry when she would leave. The fact that she was constantly running from the police didn't actually start to diminish my view of her until I was an adult. Even then, it was more of an embarrassment than anything.

Everyone knew she was a jailbird. Jail, however, was nothing compared to prison. I remember the first time she was sentenced to go to prison. She was on trial for robbery, I think. Her attorney thought it would be good for my brothers and me to be at the trial. I guess he was hoping the jury would think she needed to be home with her children. He was wrong, and my mother was convicted. When it was time to sentence her, the judge told her to stand. I think I must have been in Jr. High by that time. I was old enough to understand, but still a little unsure.

The judge read the verdict 'We find the defendant guilty', she started crying and so did I. He then sentenced her to a number of years in prison. I cried even more and couldn't stop. I cried in part because I was sad and afraid for her, but also because I was angry. I was angry with her because she had used us. She used my brothers and me to try and ease her sentence when she had never taken the time to be a mother to us. She was never there for us, but there we were, trying to save her life. I was so angry.

Once she was away, my grandmother made me write to her. My grandparents loved her more than anything, she just couldn't see it. It was as if she was still seeking attention for some reason. After a while, she and I began to correspond and things were actually going pretty well. She told me that when she got out, we were going to get our own place.

I had never in my whole life lived with my mom. My brothers would sometimes visit her in the summer; and they also lived with her during a semester one school year; but she would never let me go with them. When she wrote to me telling me I could live with her, I was so excited; I started counting the days until she would come home. I could hardly wait.

When the day finally arrived, she was released and things were great. She would take Alonzo and me out daily to look at houses. We went out almost every day for a couple of weeks. Each time, he and I would race in and choose which room we wanted. Alonzo always made it to the largest room first. Finally she settled on one she liked. She told us we would get the house, but then she left again. She didn't come back for months. When she did return, there was no mention of the new home and before long, she was gone again.

Shortly after, things returned back to our pre-prison state. Meaning, she became the wicked witch of the Panhandle again. I told her that I liked her better in prison. Actually, I wrote it in my diary and she read it. She acted like she was so hurt, but I don't know how she expected me to feel any differently. Anyway, she soon started doing things that would get her locked up again, so I had my wish quicker than I had anticipated.

Drugs have always played a major role in her life. She has always chosen not to deal with reality. I remember the first time I saw her shoot-up with cocaine. She was in the bathroom sitting on a blanket. The blanket was spread out on the floor like a picnic area. She was sitting on the floor, shooting drugs into her veins, her head would roll back. I had heard my grandfather getting on her about what she was doing in the bathroom, so I decided to look for myself.

Our house was pretty old; it had done a little settling and some of the doors didn't close properly.

The doorknob for the bathroom was fairly loose, so there was a space that allowed you to peek into the bathroom when the door was closed. I would look through the hole to see what she was doing. I wish I hadn't been so curious. Afterwards, my stomach would turn anytime she was in the bathroom for more than five minutes.

As messed up as she was, if I had to choose someone on this earth who has contributed most to my character – good and bad, it would have to be her. I never wanted to be like her. I prayed to God that He would not let me turn out like her. She was selfish and self-centered. She was always loud and drunk – stumbling over herself; and most of all, she was a terrible mother. She didn't respect herself or anyone else for that matter. Her lack of self-respect turned into self-pity.

I guess in a sense, she felt that she had been cheated. In the days of her childhood, there were no girl and boy reproductive films at school. She claims she didn't know about birth control. Once she got pregnant with my oldest brother, it was pretty much downhill for her. I am definitely not making excuses for her, but I can understand how an individual could crumble under such circumstances. As much as I wanted to be with her as a child, I realize that the Lord really blessed me by taking me away from her. I do love my mother, but had I been raised by her, my life would no doubt have been cursed. The curse that she has placed upon herself would have smothered me.

I did everything I thought would be opposite of her actions. Some of my so-called friends tried to get me to drink and smoke marijuana but I never felt pressured because I knew I didn't want to be like her. My mother was my anti-drug. I had a living, breathing billboard against drugs and alcohol right in my home.

Even more so, as much as I hate to admit it, some of her traits were still transferred to me. Her insecurities, low self-esteem even her self-pity. At some point throughout my life, I have felt each of these traits and looked in the mirror, only to see my mother's face. It haunts me like a restless spirit and I hate it. There are times when I am feeling vulnerable and worthless and each of those times, I see my mother's face. I realize that the same curse that haunts my mother lurks just beneath the surface within me.

It is a daily battle. It is a battle to convince myself that I deserve to be loved unconditionally; a battle to prove to myself that I am truly valuable to my friends and family. The good thing is that I know I don't have to fight the battle alone. My Savior has kept me through all of the turmoil – through the good days and bad days. So when I am feeling vulnerable, I know where to turn.

As messed up as she was, most people who knew her, loved her; and as hard as I tried to hate her – I loved her too. I longed for attention from her, but she didn't have time for me. She lived life in the fast lane – like she had a laundry list of things to accomplish before she died and she only had two weeks to live.

Whenever I would ask her to slow down, she would just say 'It's my life – I can do whatever I want'. Just like a defiant teenager. She always commented that she never hurt anyone – that she was only harming herself. As much as I tried to explain to her that she was hurting all of us, she refused to see the truth. She didn't want to see the truth.

Honestly, I feel that my mother resented me. When I was little, she would tell me that she had always wanted a little girl. She said that was one reason why she kept having babies. It made me feel special to hear her say the words, but as I got older, I started to wonder exactly why she wanted a little girl. Other than those words, she never made me feel special, she never took an interest in anything I did, and she never seemed to want me around. I felt that she wanted to have a daughter to abuse just as she felt she had been abused. I really think she would have loved me more if I had turned out like her. If I had gotten pregnant early and dropped out of high school – she wouldn't have had any reason to resent me.

I will never forget my eighth grade graduation. In Dimmitt, anything worth celebrating was a big deal because it was such a small town. Eighth grade graduation was my first big thing. The cool thing was that I was ranked third in my class academically. Even the principal was proud of me. He called me to his office and told me what a great job I was doing. He told me that I should be valedictorian before I graduated high school.

I was very proud and even more excited. I ran home and told my grandparents and my mother. My mom had just been released from jail, just a few weeks prior. She was never in a good mood right after she had been released. My grandmother said she would not be able to attend my graduation because she wasn't feeling well. My grandfather was tired from working all day so he wasn't going to attend either. Finally, I asked my mother, she said no because she hadn't been around for my brothers' eighth grade graduations so she wasn't going to mine.

I was so hurt, I pleaded with her, after all, she wasn't around when my brothers graduated, this time she happened to be in town. It wasn't as if she had anything else to do – she just didn't want to go and she did not go. That day, I received the Presidential Academic Fitness award, I was inducted into the National Honor Society, I received a special award for being among the top ten academic scholars in the class, I received the athletic MVP award for basketball and track and I received an award for being voted 'Best All Around' by my class.

I walked across the stage more than anyone else in the class – the principal joked about putting a chair for me on the stage. It was a very proud moment, but I would have given them all back if I could have looked out and saw my mother watching me walk across the stage to receive my diploma; but no one was there and I just smiled and thanked all of my friends' parents who congratulated me afterwards.

By the time I got home, people had already stopped by and told my grandparents about the ceremony. My mom wasn't there. I started to think she may have been angry with me for doing well. After all, she was pregnant when she walked across the stage for her eighth grade graduation ceremony. When she finally did come home, she didn't ask anything about the ceremony and I never mentioned it to her. Nothing I did was ever enough to gain her affection.

I continued to excel in school – academically and athletically. On the surface, everything looked fine. I even thought things were OK, but as I look back, I realize that even during the best of times, I was still crying out for help. Even with LD, I could get whatever I wanted from him. He always gave me money or let me use his car, even when my grandparents wouldn't let me drive theirs. I'm not sure if it was his guilt, or him trying to ease his way back in, but he always took care of me, at least financially.

I was getting attention from everyone else, but nothing from my mother. I started to drive very fast and reckless; almost as if I had a death wish. One weekend, I had LD's car, he told me not to have anyone in the car with me, but of course I picked up Sabrina. We were riding all around town. After a while, Sabrina wanted to drive, so we went out on a country road and I let her drive.

Suddenly, we hear a thump, and the road got really rough. We had a flat tire. Things did not look good. I was nowhere near where I was supposed to be. I was only eleven years old and I had never changed a flat tire. I had seen it done, so I decided to give it a try. Back then, the car jacks were a little different. They had a base and a tall stand that gradually lifted the car.

Once I got the jack in position under the car, I pulled out the tire tool and started to crank the handle, which started to lift the car. I felt relieved, when all of a sudden, the car started to slowly drop down, I couldn't figure out what was happening. Finally, I realized that I had failed to put the base of the jack on the stand and the jack was sinking deeper into the dirt road as the car sank back to the ground.

Things could not have been worse. There was no way to get the jack out of the ground and lift the car to change the tire. We were so far out in the country that it would have been dark by the time we walked into town. I wasn't really afraid, because I knew LD wouldn't give me a whipping or anything, I would just have to listen to him fuss, and I just didn't want to hear his mouth. After a while, two men came along, which was scary in itself, because we were alone on a deserted country farm road, and no one had any idea where we were. They could have done whatever they wanted to us and no one would have ever known; but God, once again, sent his angels to camp around and keep us safe. They used their jack to lift the car and pull the jack I had used from the ground. Then they changed the tire, and we were on our way. The good thing was from that point on I knew how to change a flat tire on my own.

Among the bad things was that LD had told me to bring the car back by 6:00pm. It was almost 7:00pm by the time we were on our way. So I sped into town and dropped Sabrina off at her house. In my haste, I threw the car in reverse and stepped on the gas. I backed up so fast that I felt the car jerk. I didn't realize I had hit anything, but when I tried to go forward, the car was stuck. I put it in reverse and then drive a couple of times more, trying to get the car to move, but to no avail.

Finally, my Aunt Sarah, Sabrina's mom, ran outside. She had been cooking when all of a sudden the fire from her stove went out. When she looked out and saw me, she realized that I had run over the gas meter. What she didn't realize was that I was stuck on the meter. As she got closer, she told me to turn the car off and get out. We started trying to push the car off the meter, but it was stuck.

By this time, the gas fumes were strong and a couple of other neighbors had come out to try and help. I don't know if anyone ever called the gas company, fire department or the police, but they never showed. After a while, my aunt thought she would try and drive the car off again. She climbed in and cranked up, immediately there was an enormous explosion.

God had once again protected me from harm, but my aunt had been almost completely consumed by the flames. I watched in horror as she jumped from the car and ran around, finally falling to the ground. She suffered third degree burns over most of her body. It was my carelessness that caused the accident. Eleven years old, and I had almost killed my favorite aunt.

When I went to see her in the hospital, she was barely recognizable. Her hair had been singed to her head. Her face was swollen three times its normal size and was covered with a crisp layer of black char. There were no mirrors in the room, so my grandmother had told me to act normal when I saw her; but after looking at her, how could I act normal? Knowing it had been my fault she was in such a horrid condition. She looked worse than I could have ever imagined.

My aunt was starting to feel better, so she was in fairly good spirits, but she hadn't seen herself. The doctors didn't want her to go into shock. I didn't want her to see herself. I couldn't stand to look at her. I tried to act as normal as I possibly could, but I didn't stay long. It was my fault, she was the only one who even attempted to protect me from LD, and I had done such a horrible thing to her. Even at eleven, that guilt was almost too much to bear.

I left the hospital and ran all the way home. I stayed in my room the rest of the day and cried. After that, I refused to drive. For months, I walked almost everywhere I went. If my grandmother needed me to go to the store for groceries, I would just have her take me, I would go in while she sat in the car.

My aunt was different from my mother. My mother would have taken every opportunity to remind me of the accident, but my aunt never really said anything about it. Even though she didn't say anything, I always felt an obligation to her. I always did whatever she asked. Even as I got older, I would give her my last dollar, whatever I had. Even when I knew she was abusing crack-cocaine, I would give her my last dollar. I knew why she wanted the money, although she always made up another excuse. As much as I wanted to tell her no – I couldn't turn her down. Whatever I had – she could get. I will never forget that day. I can still hear the explosion and see the smoke. I can still see my aunt turning around like a ball of fire.

One would think that would have been enough to end my stunt driving career, but once I got behind the wheel again, I went back to my reckless ways – unbelievable!

Near the gym where I played basketball, there was a small, narrow alley. The opening was just wide enough for one car. Right at the entrance was a small speed bump. If you got up enough speed, you would hit the bump and go airborne, sailing into the alley. The first time was an accident, but then it became an everyday ritual. It was extremely dangerous. There was no way to tell if another car was coming from the opposite direction. Plus, you would have to speed through an intersection to have enough velocity to hit the bump and go airborne. Even worse, there was a gas meter, only a few feet away from where the car would land. Had I hit it, the meter probably would have blown and most likely destroyed me along with the school and several surrounding houses. I admit it was one of the most stupid 'tricks' I had ever done, but I did it consistently for years.

I craved attention, and I got it. Kids would stand outside the gym and watch like I was a paid stunt person. Some would beg to ride with me. They would crouch down in the back seat- screaming the whole way; and then cheering as if I had done something good.

There was another time when a group of us were riding home from out of town; I was almost 16 at the time. It was dark and I thought I would play chicken with an oncoming car; so very careless. I had been thinking about it almost the entire trip. I analyzed the road, although it was dark, I could see that the shoulders were wide enough to accommodate a car. My plan was to pass a car in my lane as we were going up a hill, if another car started to come, instead of slowing down to get back in my lane; I was going to dart all the way across the highway to the other shoulder.

After I had worked out the 'master plan' in my head, I just did it. I started to pass a car and surely enough, another car comes along, headed straight for us. Everyone was screaming; but at the last minute, I darted across the highway to the other side and stopped on the opposite shoulder. I guess they were so happy to be alive that none of them thought enough to be angry with me.

They were all thanking me and telling me how smart I was for thinking to go to the other side. I was like a hero to them. I guess I had that same kind of charisma as my mother. Most people who knew her, loved her, even when she was stinking drunk. People were always drawn to me as well. I could have killed us all, but no one saw that. They only saw that I had save us from dying. More attention – I craved it. I guess attention was my drug.

Although I was getting attention from everyone else, my mother still had little time for me. I finally realized that nothing I did was going to earn attention from her. She was too busy seeking attention for herself. She never grew up. She never really had to – her children were being raised by other people. She felt that the money she sent was enough to make her a good parent.

I had to finally let go of that dream. I still loved her, but I was so consumed with her that it was destroying me. I could have killed myself along with countless others, but God saw fit to keep me safe once again. He sent his angels to camp around me; and I finally found the comfort I had been seeking in Him. And that comfort was greater than any other. The comfort and warmth I felt in His arms through my trials as a child and teenager sustained me. Even my mother couldn't provide that kind of safety and warmth. Finally, the need for her affection and attention subsided. I started to focus more on trying to be a better person.

Sydelle Richard

5

FORGOTTEN DREAMS

*T*he summer before my senior year in high

school, my life took an unexpected turn. That was the
summer I started dating my first real boyfriend. His
name was James Davis. Of course I already knew
him, we grew up together. Dimmitt was so small,
everyone knew everyone. He had been asking me out
for over a year, and I always turned him down. He was
very nice, but I was not attracted to him at all; but he
was VERY persistent. Another blow to his pursuit was
the fact that he was a year and a half younger than I

was, and he was three grades behind me. I hated that – he was like a little kid to me. I had to mature faster than most of the children around me, so that made him that much more immature; but he was VERY persistent; and he was so sweet to me.

The one thing he had going for him was the fact that there weren't many black guys my age in our town, and at that time, interracial dating was out. It was basically a lack of options; not to sound cruel, but it's the truth. I had turned him down more times than I could count, until one fateful Saturday. My cousin Sabrina really liked one of James's good friends named Yohance. So she convinced me to double date with them. Yohance had asked her to the movies, she asked me to go with James so that she wouldn't have to be alone. The ironic thing about our little double date was that she and Yohance got into an argument and fussed the whole night. James and I on the other hand, had a great time.

He was so funny. That was one plus he definitely had, he had a wonderful sense of humor. He could make anyone laugh. It was refreshing; I had cried so much and spent so much time being angry

that his sense of humor clouded every other strike I
had already set against him.

After that weekend, we started to talk on the
phone quite often; he was so sweet to me. I had never
had anyone be so nice to me without expecting
something in return. After a couple of weeks, I was
heading off to Girls' State. Girls' State was a summer
camp designed to give high achievers a chance to
conduct congressional business. We were all
assigned to either the House of Representatives or the
Senate. We had elections for Speaker of the House
and Senate Majority Leader. We spent days
campaigning and giving speeches. Finally, we took
real issues from our senate and debated and voted on
them in the actual state congressional houses. It was
a great experience.

Prior to leaving, James asked me to stop by
his house. He had bought me a camera, he told me to
take lots of pictures of myself and send to him while I
was gone. He thought I was beautiful; a concept which
totally threw me because I had never felt attractive. I
had always struggled with self-esteem, and here he
was telling me I was beautiful. He was gradually
drawing me in.

Things were going really well, he wrote to me while I was gone, it was so sweet. I was actually excited to get home and see him. When school started, everyone was shocked. First, because they had never seen me with anyone; secondly, because he was so far behind me grade wise. I hated that. After a while, I was ready to call it quits. I talked to my friends and I was like 'I don't really like him'; but they were saying, 'just wait until school is over, at least until after prom night.'

Keep in mind that all throughout high school I had only applied to two universities: Stanford University in California and Spelman College in Georgia. I never thought of going anyplace else. To me, getting into a serious relationship with him was senseless because he would still be in high school long after I was gone. But, I listened to my friends and continued to date him throughout my senior year.

On February 18, 1989, something dreadful happened. James and I made love for the first time. It was a Saturday afternoon. We had gone to Amarillo to my oldest brother's apartment. He was a coach at one of the high schools and we were going to watch his team play in a basketball tournament. He left to go to the gym early and we stayed behind.

After sitting there for a while, we started kissing and one thing led to another. Soon we had a blanket spread out on the floor and then it happened. The bad thing was that I wasn't sure it had happened. After what had happened to me all those years ago, I learned to basically leave my body at least mentally, so I don't really remember what it felt like. My 'true' first sexual encounter was a blur – not even real. I remember that he was extremely happy. I guess he had an orgasm, I know I didn't. From that moment on, my dreams of Spelman and Stanford slowly started to disappear.

It was true, at least for me, what they say about your first love. After we made love, it was like I was trapped. Prior to that weekend, I cared about him, probably even loved him, but it wasn't nearly as emotional as it became after that day. I know that God meant that act to be a bonding between husband and wife, so in acting those things out, it created a bond so strong, I couldn't let go.

As my senior year began to draw to a close, I fell deeper in love with James and the thought of leaving him to go to school in California or Georgia was unbearable. I couldn't leave. I was afraid of losing him. I wanted to be near him. Considering the fact that my oldest brother was the first of our family to go to college, my grandparents would not have forced me to go anywhere. They would have been just as content had I gotten a job at one of the local stores; there was no pressure for me to pursue my dreams.

I started checking into colleges closer to home and finally settled on West Texas State University. WT as it was called was in a small town about 45 miles away from Dimmitt. I could go home every weekend. In fact, I could have commuted from home if necessary. It was hard for me to leave him, but I still saw him each weekend, and sometimes during the week.

There was one of my teachers who saw my fear and encouraged me to leave, Ms. Barbara Decker. She liked James, but she thought I could do better and she told me so. She offered to drive me to Texas A&M, a larger university several hours away; anything to get me away from James. I wouldn't listen. She gave me the lecture my mother or grandmother should have given me. She only wanted what was best for me. I realize now that she was right.

Someone in my house should have made me go. I was much too young to have been in such a serious relationship. No adult in my home should have let me sacrifice my dreams for a BOY. Often we say it was just God's will, but in my opinion, a lot of the time it is our will, overriding God's will. I have no doubt that God has awesome things in store for me; but I believe that had I submitted to His perfect will, I would not have had to have taken the long road to get there. Don't get me wrong, there have been many miracles and blessings along the way, but there has also been a tremendous amount of pain and suffering as a result of my stubbornness.

By the end of my first semester, things began to change. I started hearing rumors of James seeing other people; and he started acting like a complete jerk. I was so sad, I had rearranged my life for him and he had the audacity to start tripping. He honestly treated me like crap. When I would go home, he would tell me that he didn't have time to see me, that he was hanging out with his friends. I would argue, 'You see them everyday', but he would go anyway. Sometimes I would wait up until midnight, hoping he would stop by, but most of the time he wouldn't. I cried and cried, but I never thought of leaving him.

Sometimes I would go out looking for him, but I could never find him. It would bring back memories of the times when I was in high school and everyone would be looking for him and me. He always knew the perfect spot to hide and 'park'. There was a time when his family was looking to move to a different house. Somehow he got the extra keys to the new house and we would go there on the weekends and hang out. It was only a couple of houses down from where he lived, but no one had any idea where we were. So when I would go out looking for him, I knew that if he wasn't in town, there would be no way I would ever find him.

I just could not believe he was cheating on me. I had not done anything wrong. He cheated because he could. He treated me like crap when he wanted to be with her and then he would come and make up; and yes, I let him. Once I went home for his athletic banquet. He had not mentioned it to me. One of the coaches told me about it, and since I once played sports there, I thought I would go. James was one of the star athletes so I knew he would get an award of some sort. I thought it would be a nice occasion. Boy was I wrong. When he found out I intended to go he got was irate. He told me that he did not want me there and that I was not going with him.

I could not believe how he was acting so I went to his house before the banquet. He was adamant about me not going and he left- alone. His mother saw the incident and asked me to ride with her. When we got there, I realized why James did not want me to go. As soon as I walked in the whispers began. All of James' friends were staring at me with their mouths open. Then I saw her. The girl James had been cheating with. She sat there, not making eye contact. All eyes were on her and me. I felt like a fool. Why was I so blind? The same thing happened at prom time. He started a big fight just before he left and told me he did not want me to go. I knew why. For all I know, she was his actual date.

The night he went to the prom, I stayed at his house. While he was away, I found several letters from a girl named Lucy. All of the letters ended, 'I love you'. This was more than just something casual. He had started a relationship with her right under my nose; but I had ignored all the signs.

I just wanted him to love me again. I tried to do all I could to 'win' him back. I couldn't figure out what I had done wrong to make him not want to be with me. He would tell me that he loved me, and I honestly believe that he did; but his hormones got the best of him. Every black person in Dimmitt was telling me that he was seeing other people; especially his so called friends. The main people he neglected me for, were the main ones trying to get me to leave him. These were his 'friends' whom he loved dearly, but they talked about him like a dog.

I knew in my heart that he was messing around, but I couldn't let go. I would cry and cry, but I could not walk away. I hated myself for letting him treat me that way. It always affected me internally. Instead of being angry with him and leaving him, I was angry with myself. I automatically pointed the finger at myself 'What's wrong with me?' In my mind, I was always the reason for things going wrong. I wasn't pretty enough, or smart enough; I always found something wrong with me. His actions only amplified my feelings of worthlessness. How did I let him define me for so long?

The whole time I was in college, guys asked me out all the time, but I 'had a boyfriend'. I wasted so much time, waiting on him to change. I protected him, constantly arguing and almost getting into fights with football players for talking about him. I always took up for him. Sometimes, they would say they were going to beat him up if he came to town, but I always took up for him. All the while, he was running me in the ground.

My senior year in high school was probably the best year of my life. I had finally put things of the past behind me; or at least suppressed them to the point that I could function properly. I felt good about myself. I had accomplished a lot, even though I backed out at the end and deserted my dream of leaving Texas to go to college, I was still in school. I had a job and I had earned a walk-on position on the basketball team which turned into a full scholarship. But by the end of the second semester, all of those insecurities started to come back. I was no longer confident and outgoing; I was sad and crying most of the time. All because of a BOY! It was more than that, it was because he was the only person who ever seemed to love me for me; and when he started to mistreat me, I went into meltdown mode. I would try and talk to him, but he had his own agenda and I didn't fit.

He never talked about breaking up, but why would he? He could do basically anything he wanted and still have me at his beckoning call. Why would he ever leave? I hated myself. I prayed to God for strength to leave, but I was too weak; a coward. I stayed and sank further and further into a black hole. It wasn't that I was so in love with him. It was because I had put ALL of my trust in him. When he left for college, his little girlfriend stayed behind. I thought that would be the end of the drama but I was wrong again. When I went to visit him at school, I found out that not only was he still seeing the girl back home, but he had also met someone new at school. I decided to call it quits. I broke it off with him. Finally, I came to my senses.

On top of dealing with his never-ending drama, there was another villain on the scene. Coach Sam Dimmons; he was the assistant women's basketball coach. When I applied to WT, I was going strictly for academics. I didn't want to play basketball, because I didn't feel there was a future in the sport. Little did I know that we would end up with the WNBA, but that's a different story. I had earned several academic scholarships, so that was my focus. My high school coach kept encouraging me to go and try out for the basketball team. I put him off for weeks, and finally, I decided to go. I was so scrawny, most of the girls thought I was someone's little sister. They laughed when I told them I was there to play. It was a different ball game, but I was always up for a challenge. Their comments made me work even harder.

Coach Deitz, the head coach, was impressed with me and offered me a position on the team. I was excited. Things were great. Coach Dimmons, on the other hand, was a different story. He would gripe at me the entire practice. 'King – you haven't made the team yet'. 'King – get down the court'. He hardly said a word to anyone else. He would even make me stay after practice sometimes to go over plays. I thought he was trying to make me quit. I remember calling home once and my mother answered the phone. She asked me how things were going and I told her about how Coach Dimmons was always riding my back. She told me to watch him; she said 'he probably likes you'. At the time, I thought it must have been the drugs talking. I was thinking, 'did you just hear what I said?' Anyway, I just dismissed her comments, but little did I know, those comments were probably full of the wisest advice she had ever given me.

Once the season started, Coach Deitz had placed me at point guard; I was second behind Isabel, who was a year or two older than me. He would put me in to let Isabel rest. It wasn't a whole lot of playing time, but it was consistent. Then all of a sudden, I went for weeks without touching the floor. I didn't get any playing time at all. That's when Coach Dimmons' advances started.

He first made me come to his hotel room on a road trip to watch film. I had not played at all during the game, but he made me watch film. While watching the film, he started massaging my shoulders and rubbing my back. When he tried to kiss me, I asked to leave. He made a comment saying 'you know I have a lot to do with who plays and who doesn't play.' I just looked at him and walked out. I was so pissed. I wasn't giving in to him just to play. Each week, he made more advances. He would call me, after curfew, and invite me over to his apartment; all the while insinuating that I would play more if I would give in. I hated him. I started to hate basketball. I had LOVED basketball all of my life, but he truly took away my love of the game. It was more of a job, something I had to do to pay for my education. I never said anything to anyone, because he told me I would be labeled a trouble maker; that everyone would believe him in saying I took his comments wrong. I felt he was right, so I never said a word, to anyone at home or at school.

He would always make comments to my roommate, telling her, that he would buy things for me if I would 'act right'. She would just tell me to get with him to take his money. It was more than that for me. I didn't want him to win. I didn't want his money, and after a while, I didn't care if I played. As long as my tuition and books were paid for, I was fine. Between dealing with him and my so-called boyfriend, I was struggling to hang on to sanity.

That summer, I went home, and things were ok between James and me for a few weeks, then he started again; hanging out with his 'friends' and drinking. That was the last summer I spent in Dimmitt. I never went back there to live. Partially because I had allowed him to make such a fool of me, it was embarrassing; and in part because I knew it was time to move on.

When classes started back in the fall, I had a
new attitude. Two can play his game. There had been
this guy who had asked me out for months before the
summer break. His name was Marcus Patton. He was
the only one who seemed sincere. Most of the other
guys seemed to want to get with me, just because no
one else had. It was like a competition. Marcus was
different. He was from California; he still wore a long
curl like in the movies. You know where the guy has
long curly, wet hair? There was something mysterious
about him. A lot of the girls liked him; in fact more than
I knew. I don't know why he was attracted to me. I was
really skinny and not very cute in my opinion, but
something drew him to me. We started hanging out
and he was so much fun. He made me feel special.
We had fun laughing and playing basketball, just
hanging out. I thought things were great, but
apparently, I was the only one who thought so. It
seems that Mr. Patton took a liking to one of my
teammates. I of course, was the last one to know. One
evening, I was heading to the gym for a game, I came
down the elevator in the dorms and someone said
'Hey Sydelle, I saw Marcus down here'. So off I go
looking for him, only to find him hugged up and kissing

Monica, one of my teammates. My heart sank. I could not believe it. A fool AGAIN!

I should have seen it coming. Monica had started asking me a lot of questions about Marcus. She said she liked his style, he seemed cool. I didn't think anything of it. She was already seeing two other guys; but she was notorious for 'giving up the goods' if you know what I mean. In the end, she enticed Marcus and they had been basically living together right under my nose. I had NO idea; how naïve.

When I saw them, I just looked at them both and turned away. I never said a word. They both just looked at me with their mouths open. I drove to the gym for the game, of course I didn't play – which was probably good that night. I just couldn't believe they had both been so deceptive. Why not just be honest? So now, my real boyfriend and my fake boyfriend were both cheating on me and my assistant coach was trying to get me into his bed. I was at my whit's end.

How could I talk to anyone about that? It was embarrassing. I finally told Sabrina, but she couldn't console me, how could she? It felt better just to get it out, but I still felt like a fool. Everyone knew except me. How could I be such a fool? I never suspected

anything. He was always with me, except at night-
when he was with her. He liked the way I looked and
my personality, but he had sex with her. He said it was
just a sex thing, but who knows. OK strike number
two. At that point, I didn't want another relationship.

Coach Dimmons was still on the warpath. He
actually had my roommate drop me at his house and
leave. He would pay her to watch his dogs when we
were on a road trip, so I was going with her to pick up
her money. I go to the bathroom and when I come out,
she is gone. He paid her to leave me. She didn't think
anything of it. I was so mad at her. He started trying to
kiss me. I asked him if he would leave me alone if I
had sex with him. I told him I just wanted him to leave
me alone. He said he would. So I did; at least I laid
there. I cried while he was on top of me. I was sick to
my stomach.

When he was finished, he said 'you know it
could be so much better'. I told him we would never
know because it would not happen again. I reminded
him that he said he would stop the advances if I gave
in. He asked if I was serious. He said, 'what if I was
like all the other guys and said now that I got what I
wanted, I don't want anything to do with you'. I said

'good – that's what I want you to do'. Even after that –
he would not let go.

I decided to leave and transfer to a different
school. I told my oldest brother about my dealings with
Coach Dimmons – at least about his advances. He
was furious and told me to stay, that he would take
care of the coach – but I had to leave. I did not tell
anyone at the school, primarily because everyone
seemed to like him; he was an excellent basketball
coach. He knew the game inside and out, probably
from having the players over so much 'watching film'. I
just did not want to cause trouble so I just left. I left
James. I left Marcus. I left Coach Dimmons. I didn't
want to see either of them ever again.

I transferred to a University a few hours away.
James begged me to give him a second chance. By
this time he was at school in Oklahoma. I went back to
him and things were great again for a while, but he
could never control the brain he pees out of. It
ALWAYS controlled him. I ended up breaking up with
him again. Marcus had gone back to California, he
and Monica had parted ways. Next thing I know,
Marcus Patton had enrolled at the University I was

attending. He said he came back to Texas to show me that he could be with only me. I didn't fall for that. We talked from time to time, but I wasn't going to give him a second chance to make a fool of me.

Shortly before the semester ended, I received a call from the mother of a young girl who played for Coach Dimmons at a school in New Mexico. Much to my surprise, he had left my old school when I did and gone to coach in New Mexico. Apparently, he had been harassing some of the players on his team there as well. The mother asked me if I would testify and I was more than happy to help. I still have no idea how she got my name or number, but I never heard from her again.

My senior year in college, I had one of the best coaches you could ask for, but the passion I had early on just wasn't there. I played as much as I wanted, I enjoyed it, but I was ready to move on. Graduation day was a wonderful occasion. I was proud of myself. I worked hard to get through on my own. Even in the midst of the turmoil; I prayed and I survived.

Shortly after graduation, I moved to Dallas and got a job. I hadn't been to Dimmitt in a while, but I waited until I got settled in and then went to Dimmitt for a weekend. When I got there, I found out that my grandfather was a lot more ill than I had known. He had been diagnosed with colon cancer a couple of years earlier, but each time I spoke with him over the phone, he seemed fine. He was still in high spirits, laughing and joking. When things took a turn for the worse, they went quickly. I had no idea he was as bad off as he actually was. I was devastated. I felt guilty because I had not been there. I just had no idea. I'm sure my grandmother didn't want to worry me away at school, but I wish I had known.

I returned to Dallas, quit my job and went back home. I arrived in Dimmitt on Saturday, June 12, 1993. It was two days before my grandfather's 79th birthday. I stayed inside the entire week. He was on so much medication that he was delusional most of the time. He didn't know who I was when he awoke. He looked around sort of hysterical; he had no idea who I was, that broke my heart. I stared at him crying. I stayed in his room with him, waiting for him to wake up. I felt so guilty for not being there, I wanted to do all I could for him while he was still with us. My birthday was on Friday, June 18th. By that time, James had come home for the summer, he asked me to go to dinner with him. I didn't want to leave my grandfather;

I stayed in his room with him almost all day. I would sleep beside him in a chair.

Late that night, the medication had started to wear off, and he refused to take anymore. When he woke up, he looked over and saw me. 'Rabbit?' he said. I was so happy. I wanted so much for him to know that I was there. I loved him so much and I felt I had let him down. He is the only one who saved me from that evil LD and I had not been there for him. When he called me 'rabbit', I knew that he knew who I was. I was overjoyed. I hated to see him in so much pain. He was telling me that his stomach was hurting. He kept throwing his arms up in disgust. He was so used to taking care of himself, and now he was bed ridden, unable to even walk to the bathroom. It was devastating for him to have to have someone change him and clean him because he didn't have the strength to get out of bed. I hated to see him suffer. He had been such a good man, watching him suffer seemed so unfair. I prayed for God to take away his pain.

I remember he was trying to tell me so many things, but his voice was so weak that he could hardly speak. I remember looking into his eyes, he was so sad. I told him that we would all be OK and that we would take care of Mama. I told him not to try and hang on for us. I hated to see him suffering. That was Saturday morning. That night, James stopped by and asked me to go to a movie. My family convinced me to get out of the house, since I hadn't been out the entire week. So I agreed to go. When we left that evening, my grandfather was asleep. He never awoke. As he slept, he slipped into eternal slumber. I wasn't there. The only time I left his side and he passed away, I had left him again.

As guilty as I felt, I know that God was saving me; I could not have handled the sight of him being taken away in the ambulance. I probably would have gone with him. God knew I needed to be away from the house. God also knew that I needed to have that last conversation with him, as brief as it was. I needed to hear his coherent voice once more. He slipped away shortly after midnight on Sunday morning – Father's day – June 20, 1993. Although I knew he was very ill, I never imagined him not being around. In my eyes, he was invincible. I loved him with all my heart – I wrote a poem for his funeral, at the request of my family:

Daddy, you meant the world to us
It's hard to imagine you are gone
It's so hard to picture how things will be
Since the Master has called you home

But everything happens for a reason,
So I'm sure this was for the best
If there's one thing you deserve more than
anything else,
You certainly deserve to rest

Emancipation Proclamation,
The last day of your precious life
Symbolic of the day, your soul was set free
No more heartache and no more strife

Father's Day, the day you passed on
You closed your eyes in peace
A father to many of us here below
Now our Heavenly Father you must meet

The Bible tells us there is a time for all things
Ever since time began
Now all we can do is wait and pray
Until it's time for us to meet again

That was one of the saddest days of my life. I stayed in Dimmitt for a few weeks, trying to get myself together. While I was there, James started to come around more and more. He was really supportive and caring. The night before I was to return to Dallas, James stopped by and asked me to give him one more chance. So there we were again. The third time around. I moved back to Dallas and he went back to school in Oklahoma. Once again, things were great for a while. I was also older and more mature, so I didn't let things get to me the way they had in the past. He was still doing his thing while I was away, he was a little more discreet, but I still knew.

Then, the drug use started. Actually, it may have been going on all along. He was a regular pot head and I had no idea. One weekend I went to visit, and he asked if it was ok if he smoked a joint. I just looked at him kind of strange, like 'whatever'. I stayed in his bedroom while he sat out front with some of his friends. Before I knew it, they had been smoking all day. I blew up, we had a bad argument. I left and drove back to Dallas. I didn't visit him much after that weekend.

Shortly after, I receive a call from him. He had been arrested for drug trafficking. Apparently, he and a couple of friends thought they would be drug dealers. I was pissed. I used my savings to bail him out of jail. I had just started a new job, so I had to wait until that evening to send the money; and he had the nerve to be upset because I took so long. I don't know why I didn't just run away, but I stayed. Soon, he moved to Dallas, partly I'm sure because he was too embarrassed to go back to school there in Oklahoma. Before all of the illegal activity, I had asked him to move down several times. He always told me 'No'. He did not think it would be a good idea for us to live together. That's why I'm sure he was too embarrassed to go back to school in Oklahoma. When he moved down, things were fine; he didn't smoke marijuana at all. I helped him get registered at a local university and we both started looking for him a job. Things were going well until one of his roommates decided to get away from Oklahoma. He needed a place to stay for a while, so of course, he moved in with us. Then the pot smoking started once again, and things went downhill from there. I can't say it was all his friend's fault. His friend was really a good guy. I liked him a lot, but when you put the two together, there was bound to be trouble.

Adding insult to injury, I became pregnant with my daughter. Don't get me wrong, my daughter is a wonderful blessing. I love her with all of my heart; but at the time, I could not imagine being tied to him for the rest of my life. When I got pregnant, I really just assumed that we would get married. We were already living together and it wasn't as if we had just met. We had been dating for seven years at the time. So we started planning a wedding. Midway through the process, he informs me that he never intended to get married just because I was pregnant. He said he wasn't ready. So, I called my family and friends and told them the wedding was off. I was hurt and embarrassed; but I stayed – What was wrong with me?

While I was pregnant, our relationship was at its worst; partially because of my raging hormones and partially because he was just an ass. We fought like cats and dogs; and not just arguing. We physically fought. My biggest problem was that when I was younger, I had watched my Aunt Sarah as she got beaten almost to death by her boyfriend and she never tried to defend herself. I swore that I would never let that happen to me. I may not win, but I would definitely go down fighting. I will admit that there were times that I probably irritated him to the point that he would have hit anything, but until it actually happened, I never thought he would hit me. Once he did hit me, I was like a raging bull, even pregnant, I was not going to let him think I was going to curl up in a corner and allow him to beat me.

In addition to our physical battles; his 'Mary Jane' habit was at its worst. He was high almost every day. He knew about my mother. We spoke several times about the fact that I did not want my child around drugs. He kept saying he would stop, but he only got worse. He hung out until the wee hours of the morning almost every weekend. It was terrible. We had never actually had a physical fight until I was pregnant. I lost a lot of respect for him during that time. He showed me a side of him that I had never seen; but by that time, I had convinced myself that I needed to stay because of the baby. I never knew my father and my mother was absentee as well. I wanted my child to have a family; something I never had. I thought I could stay until she was an adult. That was my intention.

After she was born, things were better for me for a while, because I would just take her and leave. We spent many nights sitting at the airport, watching the airplanes take off and land, wishing I could take her and leave. I was falling into a deep depression. I wanted to leave, but I didn't want to deprive her of her father.

When our daughter was ten months old, James proposed to me. I could tell he was nervous, he had been out of town, and the baby and I were just about to leave the house when he came in. I had been on the phone with an old friend. I was on my way out to meet him when James pulled up. He had stopped to pick up food and flowers, and he immediately got down on one knee. When I saw him kneel, my stomach started to turn. I wanted so much to say 'NO'; but I was standing there holding my daughter, and before I knew it, a soft 'yes' escaped my lips.

I couldn't believe I was such a wimp. He could tell that I wasn't overjoyed. He just kept telling me that everything would be ok. I knew in my heart that it wouldn't. I didn't love him anymore. I had lost all respect for him. His mother used to always tell me that our backgrounds were too different; meaning that he was raised in a 'Christian' environment and I was raised around drug addicts and alcoholics. I guess she had a point, but ironically enough, it was the 'holy' child who ended up on drugs. He tried to do better for a while after we were engaged, but it was short lived.

I did not want to marry him. My wedding day was more like a funeral to me. I was so sad. Sabrina tried the whole day to convince me to call things off. She knew things were not right, but I felt I had to at least try for the baby's sake. It was not all his fault. After he called off the wedding the first time, I really stop trying to work on our relationship. I was unforgiving. I didn't trust him, so we argued a lot about him staying out late. My insecurities got the best of me. Granted he was actually cheating, but I should have just let things evolve instead of stressing and starting fights. But as it was, I would press and we would end up in a shoving match which progressed into blows.

I was at the lowest point in my life. I honestly got to the point that I didn't want to live. In the past I had wondered how anyone could get to the point that he or she would consider taking his or her own life; but there I was. I didn't want to live. I was so depressed that I felt that I was doing more harm than good. My stomach was in knots with ulcers that bled. My headaches were so intense that it made me vomit. I was a complete mess. I thought my daughter would have a better life without me. My mental state was to the point that all reasonability was gone. I merely existed; I ceased to live.

Looking back, it wasn't really that important. I was considering a 'permanent solution to a temporary problem'. Don't get me wrong, things were bad, but only because I had lost sight of my Savior. I thought I was still close to Him because I still went to church and went through the motions; but had I really been where I needed to be with Him, I would have realized that He is what is most important. I wanted the marriage to work, but I didn't need to have James or the marriage. At the time however, I couldn't see that. We still fought, even with the baby. I tried to talk to him, asked him to go to counseling. He just said he didn't need anyone to tell him he had a problem. Things went from bad to worse. Women were calling the house. Some woman actually drove by and knocked our mailbox off the post. He was disrespecting me in every way imaginable. In addition, at the same time, all of the memories from my childhood came back like a stream of rushing water.

I had never told anyone and never really thought about those awful things until I got married and had a child of my own. I had a beautiful little daughter that I loved more than life. She was so beautiful and precious and I wanted to be able to protect her from all harm. It was shortly after she was born that the horror came flooding back into my mind. It was almost overwhelming. I tried to talk to James about how I was feeling. I told him everything that happened between LD and me. I wanted and needed to talk, but he would just get angry. I know he was angry because he cared about me, but he acted like he was angry at me. He wouldn't talk to me.

Next, our sex-life went out the window. I didn't want to be touched. I had emotionally detached myself from my husband because of all we had gone through while I was pregnant. So, after the baby was born and I was dealing with my emotional past, it didn't take much to take the idea of sex completely out of my mind. I would sometimes try and force myself to make love to him, but he knew it was 'forced' and he would get angry. I really thought counseling would have helped us both deal with all of our issues, but he hated the thought of 'getting someone else in our business' and he refused to go.

I started to think about everything LD had done and all he had robbed me of. He stole my innocence of childhood. He made me behave as a grown woman when I was only a child. I hated him. I hated him for the way my eyes always looked sad even when I was smiling; because they held behind them an ugly and disgusting secret that turned my stomach inside out. I hated him because I could never experience a true first kiss with someone I loved without thinking of my real first kiss with him. I hated him because the first time I made love to someone I truly loved, I had thoughts of my first orgasm with him. I hated him so much so that it began eating away at my very core.

I decided that I needed to confront him. I drove to his house late one night, on my way to Dimmitt. When I walked in, he spoke as usual. I asked him why he had done those things to me. Initially, he denied the whole thing, which made me even more upset. He kept asking me who was filling my head with those ideas. He said he knew it was my Aunt Sarah who had been telling me such things. I told him that I remembered everything he had done to me. Finally, he apologized, but it was more like he was apologizing for me being upset, he never admitted anything. He just said that what ever he had done, he realized he was paying for it now because he was really sick and things had gotten to be really hard for him financially. He said he was sorry for what ever he had done to me. He asked me not to mention anything about it to anyone else. He was more concerned with what people would think about him than all the pain he had caused me. I was so disgusted. I just got in the car and drove away. I never saw him again after that night. Last I heard he was near vegetable state in a nursing home.

That night, I went on to my grandmother's house and my mother was there. My mother and I had never really had a relationship, but that night, I really needed to talk, so I told her what had occurred. I told her about how long the ordeal lasted and how I somehow blocked it out for years. Immediately, her tears began to flow. I could tell that she was really emotional. When she finally composed herself enough to speak, she told me that he had tried to do the same thing to her. When she said that, my heart sank. Why would you leave your only daughter there as live bait for a man you knew was not fit to be around any child, especially a female? All I could think of was protecting my precious little daughter from all the pain that I had endured and yet I find that my own mother left me to fend for myself in the lion's den. Of all the heartless things she had done to me as a child that topped everything.

After a while, I started to wonder if maybe my grandmother had known what had been going on all those years. Several of my school mates had teased me about it, even my Aunt Sarah had questioned me, but my grandmother never said a word. Why had she not ever questioned his motives? Why did she continue to let me spend so much time with this man? Why was he always giving her money for me 'helping' him? I never asked my grandmother those questions, because had she not been involved, I didn't want to hurt her feelings. Deep down, I felt that she knew, and maybe I just didn't want the confirmation from her. When I told her about the things he had done, she just said 'that was a long time ago and now LD is an old man, just leave it alone'. She never got angry or upset; in fact, she invited him down just a couple of weeks later. I feel that they probably had a conversation about me, but I never asked the questions, so I will never know the real truth.

My grandmother was really money driven when we were young. She once told me that all I would have to do was sit on Mr. Dickson's lap for him to give me money. I just looked at her. I could not stand to look at Mr. Dickson, much less sit on his lap – I didn't care how much money he had. It was her comments such as that which made me question her knowledge and even her motives with LD. My question was why? I often wondered what her childhood must have been like. It is hard to imagine it was pleasant based upon her actions as an adult. She never talked about her life as a child. Was she molested as well? Was that what she considered normal? I will never know. I do know however, that she loved me. Regardless of her actions, motives and even her words – she did love me.

Besides that, the thought that my mother had basically fed me to the wolf so that she could live her selfish lifestyle added to the animosity that was already present in our estranged relationship. I could barely stand to look at her and usually if I called and she answered the phone, I would just hang up. I couldn't stand to hear her voice. I didn't have a decent conversation with her for about a year. In fact, I distanced myself from just about everyone for quite some time.

I felt as if my whole life was falling apart. My marriage was in ruins, and felt I had been used by my grandmother, the one person I loved most. My mother was more of a drug head than ever. Things were spinning out of control. I tried to reach out to my husband but he was so involved in his marijuana and his other women that he didn't have time to listen to me. I went to his job one day; I told him that I really needed to talk to him. He walked away. He went into the office and I sat in the car and cried. That day, I decided that I was going to leave this earth. I took the baby to daycare and kissed her good-bye. I went home and took out a bottle of pain medicine. I got my bible out and read Philippians chapter 4. After I read, I prayed, I told God that I was tired, and that I would rather be in Heaven, I told him that if he wanted me to stay here that he was going to have to do something and do it quick, because my every indication was that this was no place for me. I was tired of being hurt, I was tired of being betrayed, I was just tired of being in pain. After I prayed, I went into the kitchen to get a glass of water, and walked to the bedroom with the pills.

The moment I started to open the pill bottle, I heard the front door open. My husband had come home. Initially, I thought he had gotten a message from God too and was coming to tell me that we could go to counseling. I was actually excited for a brief moment until he came into the room and started ranting and raving and cussing me like mad for showing up at his job. Not quite the sign I was looking for, but it stopped me from opening the pill bottle. At that very instant, I knew I had to get out. The person I was with was sacrificing the person I was meant to be.

I just started praying. I knew that God would listen any time of day or night. I prayed that I could just forget everything that had happened; but God said 'no'. I had to learn to cope first and then conquer. It was a recovery phase; but there was a definite purpose behind my pain. I asked God to help me to want to live for me. For most of my life, I had lived for someone else. When I was younger, I knew that my grandmother would be sad if I were to die. After I had my daughter, I knew that she needed me. That kept me going. It's amazing that God saw fit to keep me even when I didn't want to be kept. He always gave me a reason to keep going. I prayed that for once I would want to live for myself; because I wanted to live my life, not because of someone else.

I asked God to strengthen me and to especially guard my baby's mind and heart so that she would be shielded from any negativity that I may have brought. I desperately wanted my marriage to work, but after a while, I had to stop obsessing over the fact that I had failed and start trying to regain my grip on reality. The truth of the matter was that my marriage ended the day or night he chose to lie down in another woman's bed. Our covenant had been tainted at best, but ultimately broken. He had already ended our marriage. I just needed to let go. The problem I had was that although he had completely disregarded his covenant with God, I knew that I had also made a covenant. Yes, he had cheated and no, I should not have gotten married in the first place, but I still made that vow before God and man. By man's standard, I was justified in filing for divorce, but I felt that I had let my Father down. He knows all things, so He knew it would happen; the good thing is that he also knows my heart and how much I long to please Him. I made a mistake, it wasn't the first or the last and I know that he has forgiven me. It just took me a while to forgive myself.

With LD, I finally realized that the only way I would ever be able to get over all he had done, would be to forgive him, and more importantly, let myself off the hook. I had carried so much guilt around for so many years that I finally had to convince myself that it wasn't my fault. He took advantage of me as a little child. He was wrong, but I had to forgive him. Time and time again, I had asked God to forgive me for whatever I had done to deserve the things that had happened to me.

I know now that the enemy was attacking me. I know that he wanted my soul. He wanted to steal my joy and turn me away from the Lord; but all he did was increase my faith. He meant it for evil, but God made it ALL GOOD. I had spent many years feeling sorry for myself. Having my own little pity party, and one day the Lord spoke to me and I realized that it was more of a blessing than a curse. God thought I was worthy enough to stand the trials. Just as he told Satan to consider his servant Job, God chose me.

It wasn't a curse, it was an honor. Job had done nothing wrong, God knew that Job would not stop serving and worshipping Him no matter what. Somehow he saw that same resilient spirit in me. As hard as my life has been, I am thankful for the trials as much as for the blessings. The trials brought me closer to Him. It wasn't my accomplishments, but my failures and trials that allowed me to grow the most; and now that I have grown in Christ, I have no doubt that I would go through it again; especially if it meant saving another child from having to suffer. God never changes, the same God that took care of me then still watches over me today; and if he asks who will go, I will gladly reply 'Lord send me'. I thank God that he found me worthy.

After the conversation I had with my mother, my views of her definitely changed. I was hurt. I felt that she had behaved selfishly. I kept trying to convince myself that she really loved me; but the more I thought about the situation, I felt there could be no way that she had any love for me. How could she? When I look at my child, I get choked up just imagining her facing kids on the playground. I want to protect her from everything. I want to shelter her so that she will never have to feel the pain I felt. I don't want her to feel any heartache. I know that I can't possibly protect her from all harm, but as her mother, I feel responsible to do all I can to cushion her falls.

At her daycare facility, they asked each parent to bring a picture of his or her child and write a brief note telling the child how we feel about him/her. Just to let the little one know that he or she is special. Needless to say, my note turned into a short story. It just wasn't something I could express in one or two words. My little girl was the love of my life; my joy and my inspiration; everything to me. A tiny little body that houses an enormously energetic and bright young child. So full of innocence, so free and uninhibited. All that I long to be. I watch her and wish that for one day I could have her same perspective on life. She gives her all in everything she does and she does really well.

I cannot express how much she has changed my life. I definitely think that every woman should experience motherhood for herself. When I talk to my childless friends about being a parent; they never quite understand, because you cannot convey the feeling through words. You cannot explain to a person without a child how it feels to see pictures of missing or murdered children and wonder if anything could be worse than fearing your own child is dead; or how it brings tears to your eyes at night because you suddenly realize that you cannot protect them from all harm. Just the sheer inner happiness in watching them sleep so peacefully, knowing that you provide at least one safe haven for them; or the innocent way they reach for you to hold them when they are tired or afraid. There are no words to express these feelings.

Not that it is all joy, I can remember the first time I took her to the mall and she didn't want to hold my hand; or when she threw a fit in the grocery store because she couldn't have candy, I just spanked her right there in the store, of course I felt like Evileen the Wicked Witch of the West when it was over, but I did it, for her own good. I guess the point is, you have to take the bad with the good; but for me, the good far out-weighs the bad. I would not trade her for the world. She is a very unique being and I love all of her; the bossy, the shy, the cranky, the sugar-sweet and the spoiled rotten. She is mine and I adore her. Children are a blessing and a precious resource that so many of us take for granted. I hope that I never become that person. I hope I never take her for granted, but each day show appreciation for being blessed with such a healthy, vibrant and beautiful child.

I hope that I show her and tell her each day how important she is to me and to the world. I do not know what she is destined to become. What ever she decides to become, I have no doubt that she will be a great success. The thought that is really humbling is that although so many parents bask in the glory of their children's accomplishments, their destiny is already set, by no will of our own. So no matter what I would like for her to become, it is out of my hands. All I can do is offer her a support system of values and morals, self-respect and self-esteem and sit back and watch God do His work. It is a joy that is so real, it actually hurts. I love her so much, I couldn't imagine intentionally causing her harm; my mother on the other hand, I feel like she took me to the highest cliff and pushed me over the edge. Glory be to God that He sent His angels to cushion my fall.

OPEN DISCUSSION

Shortly after my mother was released from

prison in 1999, she was required to enroll in a

substance abuse program. It was a psychology based

program. The counselors suggested that my brothers

and I come to one of her sessions. The meeting

request was two-fold; first, to give us somewhat of a

progress report on our mother; secondly to allow her

to express some of her emotions which in turn would

help her to confront the issues and ultimately get

beyond them.

I really didn't know what to expect. At the time, I had been talking to her regularly. My grandmother had recently passed away and she seemed to be trying to turn her life around. She told me that she had learned a lot from the counselors and she was starting to realize that her addiction was a disease.

When my brothers and I arrived, we met the counselor and introduced ourselves. He began by telling us about addiction and how the process of recovery works. I had read enough about the disease to know that we were about to embark on a lifelong voyage; especially since my mother had struggled with the addiction for so long. The counselor asked us to each speak candidly with our mother, telling her how we felt. He wanted us to get everything out in the open. I remember sitting there as if in a trance, listening to my brothers. My oldest brother spoke first. He said that he remembered her being a loving and nurturing mother when he was very young. I was floored. He said the only problem was that she was never around. I never remembered her as loving or nurturing. I honestly can't recall her telling me she loved me; at least not as a child. I couldn't believe what I was hearing. He is five years older than me, so maybe during the first few years she actually functioned as a mother.

When he asked me to speak, I told him that I didn't remember the loving mother. I told him that I never felt that she loved me at all. The entire time I was speaking, she just stared at me, a blank stare, not loving or even angry, just a blank stare. I told them all of the things LD had done. Outlining specific details, and telling them how I resented my mother for the things that had happened. I went into all of the gory details, but she never flinched. She never turned away or showed any emotion. The ironic thing was that when my brother was speaking, she was crying like a baby. The counselor asked her why she cried so much when my brother was speaking and yet when she listened to the horrible account of my childhood, she never shed a tear. She said that my brother really seemed to be hurting and that she had already come to terms with what had happened to me. She said that she already knew about the things that happened to me, but she didn't realize how much my brother had been hurting. I am not sure how you cry for one child and not for the other when they are both in pain. I don't know if I will ever reach the threshold where it doesn't hurt anymore. I will never forget that day. I learned a lot about my mother, my brothers and myself.

There was so much turmoil in my life at that time. Within a matter of months I had left my husband on a 'trial separation'. I had started a new job, lost my grandmother and experienced a multitude of emotions regarding my mother. I was closer to God than I had ever been. I had to be, no one else could have brought me through. As rough as things were, and as many times as I wanted to give up, when it was all said and done, I wanted to live for me. Even more so, I wanted to live for Christ. I wanted to make Him proud of me. I realized that I had an important place in this world. There aren't many people I know who have endured the things I have gone through and lived to 'Praise' about it. I prayed for forgiveness for my mother and for LD. Ultimately, I prayed for their salvation. I think that was the key. Never before had I prayed for God to save their souls, once I did, I'm sure God was thinking 'she finally got it'. I was free. Don't get me wrong, there are still some days that try my soul, but never to the point that I even consider taking my own life. There are days when I'm looking up for any sign that Christ is coming, thinking 'Lord – today would be a good day for you to return'; but ultimately, I am thankful for life. It is a gift that I took for granted, and I promised God that I would never make that mistake again. I will spend the rest of my life spreading the Good News. I will tell everyone every chance I get about my God; the God who saves; the God of forgiveness; the God of peace. I love Him with every fiber of my being.

Sydelle Richard

7

LETTER TO MAMA

I still have a few unresolved feelings,

especially about my grandmother. I have a lot of
questions that I will never be answered, because
when I get to Heaven, I'm not trying to rehash
anything from the past. A lot of people say they will
ask loved ones specific things when they see them in
Glory – not me. Just give me my dancing shoes. And
as much as I would like to think that she is watching
over me, there are parts of me that hope she isn't. I
wouldn't want her to see the turmoil that is going on

down here. I wouldn't want her to be worried about decisions I make. I want her to just walk around and marvel in the glory of the Lord. So while I'm here on earth, I'll continue to pray and sort things out as I go. Things were difficult for so long, and I didn't feel I could talk to anyone; that's when I began to write. Writing allowed me to get some things off my chest and release some tension.

Dear Mama,

I am so sorry I didn't tell you that I loved you. I wanted so much to make you proud of me. I just had so many hang-ups that I could never quite communicate my feelings. You and Daddy were such a blessing; and honestly, I tried to keep that in mind as I was growing up. I know I was a handful when I was younger, but as I got older, I realized that you two had taken on a tremendous burden in raising me. You were almost sixty years old when I was born. I couldn't imagine the same task.

I have so many things I want to say and my mind is racing around at 100 miles per hour so please bear with me. I just can't believe that you are gone. It can't be true. I spoke with you just days ago. This has to be a dream, a nightmare. Someone must be playing an awful trick. Please please please wake up. Please talk to me. Please hug me. You said you were coming to stay with me.

You are supposed to help me get through my divorce. You are supposed to be here. Please wake up. You cannot leave me. You are all I have. I have no one left without you. You have been my courage. I was never afraid because I knew that you were always in my corner. You were always on my side. You just helped me make one of the most crucial decisions of my life and now you are gone. Why? Why didn't I get to say goodbye? Why didn't I go and pick you up instead of having you wait for a ride? Why didn't I call just a few hours earlier? At least I could have heard your voice just once more. Please wake up and talk to me. I love you. I love you. I love you. I am so sorry I never said it. On top of that, I forgive you. I held on to resentment for the last few months of your life. It was eating away at me and our relationship suffered because of it. I forgive you for everything that happened with LD. I forgive you for all of the dirty old men that came into my life. I forgive you for whatever else may have been eating away at you before you passed on. I have always loved you. I wanted to make you proud of me, but now it is too late. In my heart, I know that you were proud of me no matter what. I just had big dreams and ideas, and I had to get things done 'right now', so I didn't spend as much time with you as I should have. I was too busy trying to make things happen, that I lost sight of what was really important. I wish a thousand times that I could go back and relive even the last week with you. I want you to know how special you are to me. I tried to show you in my own way, and I am sure that you knew, but things are so different now. My views and my attitude have completely changed. I am starting to learn to cherish the people most important in my life. I am finally starting to love even myself. I have hated Sydelle for most of my life. I have felt ugly and dirty and unworthy of being loved, by you or anyone else. That's one reason it has always been so hard for me to say the words 'I love you'. I didn't know what real love was; and I didn't feel loved.

Through much prayer and dialogue with the Lord, I have come to know what it feels like to be loved. His love for me has allowed me to grow and in turn show true love to those around me. I am still trying to find out who my real father is. I'm not sure I will ever know the truth. I have finally moved on, I have a new husband and a beautiful baby boy. You would love them both and they would love you as well. I promised you that I wouldn't let my daughter forget you, and I won't. I still show her your pictures and make sure she knows who you are. Once the baby is older, I will tell him all about you, so once we get to Glory – he will already know who you are.

I actually feel closer to the family. I have never felt that I could lean on anyone, but my brothers have shown me more love and support than I could ever imagine. I am so thankful for them. You always wanted us to have a loving relationship, and finally, you have your wish. Even my mother; I have always loved her. There have been many days that I didn't LIKE her very much, but I have always loved her. I don't know that she has ever loved herself. I'm not sure that she loves herself even now; but because of my spiritual growth, I can look past her addictions and see the real person –Satchell. I can accept her and love her, even with all of her flaws. I can love her in spite of all we have gone through. In essence, I can love her in spite of herself. I can do that because God has loved me in spite of myself. He knows all about me; the good and the bad; and he has never turned his back on me. He has always loved me; long before I loved Him and even longer than before I began to love myself. I doubt that she and I will ever have a true 'mother/daughter' relationship, but hopefully one day we will be friends. I know that you desperately wanted us to be close. I'm trying

Mama. I'm still trying to make you proud. I love you.
See you in Glory.

Sydelle

NEW BEGINNING

*A*fter I wrote the letter, I sat and cried. I cried because I missed her. I cried because I was angry. I cried because I felt so alone. It was the day of my grandmother's funeral and I was completely numb. I loved her so dearly, but the more I examined my situation, the more I started to realize that not only was she aware of my ordeal with LD, but more than likely, she orchestrated it. Her main focus was money. She had made comments about me flirting with the older men for money. On top of that, had she not been involved, there is no way LD would have gone to her house shortly after I had confronted him. She didn't have any reaction when I told her all that happened. She just told me to leave it alone.

I didn't want what I believed to be the truth to taint my memories of her. The day of the funeral, I tried to focus on happier times. Mama didn't give her life to Christ until very late in life. She was well into her seventies before she started to attend church. I could not imagine living the majority of my life without a personal relationship with Christ. But she did. Honestly, that fact alone made it easier for me to forgive her. It isn't an excuse. There is no valid excuse for basically 'pimping' your seven year old granddaughter. I can not justify it, but I can and have forgiven her.

It was not easy. I was hurting and angry. I started to ask questions but, the more questions I asked, the more pain I felt. The more pain I felt, the more I wrote. I continued to add to her letter until I could finally say 'I forgive you'. The original letter was full of pain and regret. Over the years I have been able to replace some of the hurt with healing and some of the anger with joy. I spoke with Satchell, and she told me stories of my grandmother encouraging her pursue much older men. The bottom line was, my grandmother was out for money by any means necessary; but my love for her remains the same.

My heart was heavy. I knew that I still loved her and would always love her. I had to find a way to let go of the anger. The hurt is still there, but the anger was eating away at me. I first had to find myself. I had been a people pleaser all of my life. I never took the time to get to know me. I didn't know where to begin. I started to feel sorry for myself. I had lost both of my parents. At least the two people I knew as parents. I was struggling with the anger I felt toward my Grandmother; I didn't feel I could share those feelings with anyone. Then late one night, I was watching television and there was a minister on, Bishop TD Jakes. His topic was 'Forever the victim'. He spoke about how some people go through life crying 'woe is me'. He basically said that it was ok to mourn but at some point you have to get over 'it'; whatever 'it' is. He said you have to resolve within yourself that you are not a victim, but a victor. Regardless of what you have been through, if you went through it, it means you are still here and that's victory. Most people who knew me, probably did not even sense that I was playing the victim; but after that night, I knew that I was. I was feeling sorry for myself. I took every opportunity for pity. Anytime anyone felt sorry for me, it made me feel better; until that night.

After hearing that sermon, I decided that I was not going to continue to live as a victim. I was victorious and for me to continue to live in sorrow meant I was allowing Satan to win. That night my paradigm shifted. I gave up my sorrow and searched inward for joy.

I searched inward for me. Not only did I not know who I was, I seemed to have forgotten whos I was. Meaning, I was a child of God, I belonged to Him. That fact alone was enough to celebrate victory. I started to spend a lot of time in meditation and bible study. I claimed to be a Christian, but what did I really know about Christ? I began to study Mathew, Mark, Luke and John of the Bible. These books are known as the Gospels of Jesus Christ. I wanted to know the very heart of Jesus. I spent time trying to learn as much as I could absorb about my Lord and Savior. Several times, I had heard ministers say that 'Someone prayed for you, that's why you are here today'. I always wondered, 'who in the WORLD prayed for me?' After reading the Gospels, I knew. John chapter 17 tells me that Jesus himself prayed for me. He prayed for himself, He prayed for His disciples and He prayed for all of us who would come to know Him. How deep is that? Jesus prayed for me. That was enough. I didn't know one other person on earth who I thought would pray for me, but just knowing that the awesome, wonderful redeemer and savior prayed for me was all I needed.

I also fell in love with the book of Philippians. The book of Philippians is a book of encouragement. Paul, the author is in prison but his message is positive and powerful. In Philippians Chapter four, Paul tells us to keep our thoughts positive. He teaches us that the secret of being content in any situation is to know that we can do all things through Christ. I believe that I can do anything with Christ Jesus. Just knowing that allowed me to be free. Free to give and receive love. Free to laugh. Free to be me.

I spent a large portion of my life trying to over-compensate for all of my shortcomings; my low self-esteem; my insecurities, even my self-pity. I was trying to compensate by becoming an over-achiever, a perfectionist. No one on this earth is perfect and no one will be until Jesus returns. I felt that I had to earn the love of my friends and family, consequently, I ended up getting used time and time again. There aren't many people in the world who can handle a person as giving as I am and not take him or her for granted. So I had to learn that love isn't something you earn by being perfect. My love grew out of my relationship with the Lord. His unchanging, unconditional love taught me to love myself; and with that, I learned to accept love from others. Don't get me wrong, to this day, it is still a process I am going through, but it is getting better and easier with time.

One of the most important lessons I have learned throughout all of my sufferings is that it is not my fault. Things didn't just happen because I was a bad person. Granted, there have been times when I got myself in trouble following my own agenda and yes, there was suffering; but I wasn't molested because I was a bad person. I wasn't paying for any past sins. What I realize now is that as Christians, suffering is inevitable. Jesus Christ suffered and He was without sin. He is the only begotten son. If He was persecuted and endured pain, why should we expect anything different? Why should we complain? First Peter tells us that we should be prepared to suffer if it is necessary in doing God's will. And you know what? I don't mind. A lot of my friends ask me how I can stay positive when so much is going on, for me it is simple: I finally realize that the fight is fixed. No matter what happens, God is ultimately in control; and whether it is here or on the other side, I can already claim the victory. I heard people say that all my life, and I never received it into my spirit; but now that I have, I no longer fight with uncertainty, doubt or fear because I know that I know that I have already won.

It is my hope that my story helps someone. Someone who is living in the past. Someone who has been hurt by someone you love. Someone who has lived his or her life afraid to trust. I was that person. I held on to resentment so long that I almost lost everything. I lost my first marriage, but that was something I chose, not what God chose for me. I lost countless numbers of precious moments with my family. I was angry with my mother. I spent a number of years trying to get her to go into rehab or some sort of counseling; but it was more for my sake than hers. I wanted her to be a mother to me. At the time, I felt I needed her to be a mother. I could never see past her addictions. I couldn't see Satchell the person because my view was clouded by the drug addict and the alcoholic. What if God looked at us and never saw past our faults? What if He only saw our flaws and loved us only according to what He could see on the outside. We are often quick to judge one another by what is on the outside, but thank God that He loves us in spite of ourselves, inside and out.

I had to learn to do that with my mother. I had to search long enough to find Satchell, the being, not the drug addict or the alcoholic. I try now to live by example. I want her to see Christ in me. Christ is not judgmental. I try not to judge her. Christ's love is unconditional; I love her even when she is drunk. I am learning to hold my tongue; and I pray for her instead of constantly telling her everything she is doing wrong. John 3:16 is always a popular verse to recite. It states that 'For God so loved the world that he gave his only begotten Son, that whosoever believeth in Him shall not perish, but have eternal life'. I love that verse, it is very powerful, it clearly demonstrates God unconditional love for us. The problem with the popularity of the verse is that many people stop there, instead of reading on.

The very next verse, John 3:17 states that 'For God sent His son into the world, not to condemn the world, but that the world through Him might be saved.' How deep is that? If Jesus himself, who is perfect, can overlook our spots and blemishes and not pass judgment on us, who are we to judge one another? The bible tells us to be fishers of men, drawing them unto the kingdom of God, but many Christians have the misconception that the fish come out of the ocean already clean. So instead of embracing our sisters and brothers who don't know Christ, we push them away by passing judgment before they have a chance to get to the alter.

I want to mimic Christ. I believe that whatever situation he places me in, he is using me that someone may be saved. That someone today, just may be my mother Satchel. I honestly pray that one day she will be able to look in the mirror and see what God sees; that she will be confident enough to face the world and all of its problems instead of hiding from them in a needle or a bottle. I love my mother. I have always loved her; I know now that she loves me as well. She has always loved me.

It seems that after all of these years, even with the horrible memories of the past, I feel brand new. Even though I still have the memories of the past, they are not as painful. I am closer to my family than I have ever been; my brothers, my cousins and yes my mother. For once in my life, I feel that I have a true family; definitely non-traditional, but a family none the less. People I can depend on. I have never been able or willing to reach out to others for support of any kind – until now. I feel like Job in chapter 42 – the last chapter in the book of Job. God restored everything Job had lost – even more abundantly than before. I have a new family. I have my husband; my daughter who is such a phenomenal little being – smart, beautiful and ALREADY spiritual!!!; my son, my sweet little butterball; I am excited just waiting to see all of the things he will accomplish. I have truly been blessed.

So trust me, regardless of what you are going through or what you have gone through in the past, I speak from experience in saying that if you know Christ, it will be all good. You may be hurting, you may have been betrayed, you may feel there is no way out, but if you just hold on to God's hand, and even when you can't seem to trace His hand continue to trust His heart, knowing that He knows what is best; and He wants you to have the best; when you come out on the other side – you'll look back and know that although your enemies meant to hurt you, they meant it for evil, but because of your hook up with Christ – IT'S ALL GOOD! Be strong my friends!

Sydelle Richard

Edited By: Glory Books Publishing, LLC

Cover Photos: Memories by Courtney

Published by: Glory Books Publishing, LLC

P.O. Box 2373   214.868.8017

Cedar Hill, Texas 75106   www.dearmamaonline.com

ABOUT THE AUTHOR

Sydelle Richard is a gifted writer who has won numerous awards for her poetry. She is a motivational speaker who continuously captivates and inspires audiences. An advocate for health and fitness, she serves as a member of the African American Outreach Task Force for the American Heart Association. She is devoted to mentoring young girls and women. Sydelle is married with two beautiful children.

For more information on Sydelle Richard's speaking engagements, or to book her for your event, please contact her at:

Sydelle Richard

Phone:
214.868.8017

Website:
www.dearmamaonline.com

Email:
srichard@glorybookspublishing.com

Sydelle Richard

Dear Mama

Printed in the United States
61991LVS00001B/103-135